BLAME
THIS BOOK

**Rescue Your Workplace Culture
From Toxicity & Scapegoating**

DUSTIN STAIGER

Library of Congress Cataloging-in-Publication Data
Name: Staiger, Dustin, author.
Title: Blame this book: rescue your workplace culture from toxicity & scapegoats / Dustin Staiger.
Identifiers: ISBN 979-8-9877814-0-1
Subjects: Workplace Culture, Leadership & Motivation, Business Management, Human Resources

BlameThisBook.com

Printed in the United States of America
Set in Minon with Monserrat

Book design by Fredrick Haugen

Table of Contents

Foreword

There's a commonly-used story of a couple of fish swimming in a pond. Another fish crosses their path and says, "Good morning, gang! How's the water?" As he is swimming away from them, the pair of fish look at each other as one asks, "What the hell is water?"

It's hard to sense the influence culture has on us when we are in its midst. During the COVID-19 pandemic, when the office was off-limits for many workers, the crisis created distance between us and the culture in which we were swimming. We became aware of the 'water' that surrounded us at work. As the pandemic's severity lessened, many workers decided they didn't want to return to that water. They found a different pond with a healthier milieu or never dipped their toes back into any pond.

One reason many opted out was the hostility they experienced from their leaders or teammates. Within an article in the *MIT Sloan Management Review*, a survey by Revelio Labs revealed that a toxic work culture was the leading reason for workers leaving their job during the depths of the pandemic, a phenomenon dubbed The Great Resignation. In fact, toxic work culture was more than ten times more important than compensation in their decision to leave.

'Seeing the water' affected more than those who didn't return to the office. Some workers came back physically but not fully in spirit, a movement that pundits framed as 'quiet quitting.' The NPR radio show *Planet Money* asked their audience to share their thoughts why they worked half-heartedly.

> *"I leave my office at the end of the day, not thinking about what I need to work on when I go home... I do not feel anxiety when it comes to requesting time off, taking personal days, or especially taking sick time."*

> Sara M., department manager

So, even if everyone in your team returned to the office, they may have disengaged from putting in any extra effort. Some needed this adjustment for their mental health. Others chose it because they recognized that their work culture was toxic.

We now have the opportunity to transform our workplace cultures. That thought may scare you more than it inspires you. But as former U.S. Army Chief of Staff, General Eric Shinseki, once said, "If you don't like change, you're going to like irrelevance even less."

The Terminator

Arnold Schwartzenegger is an excellent example of someone who embraced change. As a bodybuilder, Arnold is still considered a legend. However, advances in the sport have introduced many who've surpassed his physique. Schwartzenegger is unique because he became a household name after his transition into acting.

Yet, he could have relied on muscle-bound action roles like his breakthrough, *Conan the Barbarian*. Instead, the Terminator took on comedic parts such as *Twins*, *Kindergarten Cop*, and *Jingle All The Way*. Eventually, the Austrian pivoted again—taking a cue from his hero, actor-turned-politician Ronald Reagan. He campaigned to become the next Governor of California. As you may know, he won and served two terms.

Arnold recognized shifts in the relationship between his career and the market. A similar change has occurred across the business landscape. Talented workers realize they don't have to return to an unhealthy work environment. Customers, vendors, and suppliers want to do business with companies that value their workforce and cultivate win-win relationships.

The bad news

We're all addicted to blame, and it has made our workplaces toxic. And if we don't find a way to detox and recover our cultural health, the consequences will only worsen as the stakes increase.

For many, the workplace is a collection of hostile and self-serving individuals. It's my thesis that this trend is the product of a vicious cycle of blame spiraling out of control.

The good news

A transformation is happening. Some leaders see an opportunity and are cultivating places where everyone can bring their best selves to work. In these forward-thinking companies innovative ideas thrive, and solutions are more important than finger-pointing or avoiding responsibility.

These organizations weathered The Great Resignation without losing their best teammates because they learned to create fulfilling work while nurturing healthy interpersonal relationships.

You can do the same. In this book, I share:

- Why the blame habit is so addictive
- The signs of a blame culture
- Practical steps to empower creativity and innovation
- How to create accountability without blame

This book is about transforming the foundation of our culture. We can break the vicious, addictive downward spiral of blame and trade it for a virtuous cycle instead.

The transformation is happening. Leading yourself, your team, or your organization through this revolution requires change. *Blame This Book* will help you navigate away from the rocks of irrelevance.

Whether swimming in a corporate ocean or a startup pond, you can intuit the water surrounding you. You'll gain an awareness to decide whether you like where the water is heading—whether you will go with the flow, swim against the tide, or be a force that changes the water itself. And, you can lead others to do the same.

Then you can say to your fellow fish, "Good morning, gang! The water is great!"

PART 1

Why Blame?

1

"Blame is for God and small children."

Dustin Hoffman
as Louis Dega in the film *Papillon*

The
Blame Loop

Adam & Eve

Blame began when, as Milton wrote, Paradise was lost.

The Garden of Eden is described as a literal paradise. As the creation story goes, all was well until God created the first people, Adam and Eve. Then things got interesting. The human pair could partake of any fruit in the garden except for one tree. As you may already know, they ate that forbidden fruit. This ancient and inaugural instance of reverse psychology was a major infraction. God wanted answers.

According to the tale, Adam and Eve were the only people in existence. Obviously, they had no one else to blame. Of course, they would take responsibility for their actions, right?

No, they did not. The buck did not stop with Adam.

Instead of taking responsibility, he blamed Eve for giving him the fruit. So Eve was stuck with the blame. But just when you think there's no possible solution, she blamed a serpent for tricking her.

This is the first human-centered story in the Christian Bible. It appears in the Jewish Torah and the Muslim Quran as well. These three Abrahamic religions represent roughly 55% of the global population. Why is this story of a tragic choice in Paradise and avoiding blame found in the root beliefs of more than half the world?

Because it's in all of us.

Whether it was famines, floods, or invasions by neighboring armies, early tribal cultures often looked for someone to blame. Those saddled with the burden of guilt were exiled, or an innocent bystander was sacrificed to appease the gods.

While this sounds like ancient superstition, we still play this game today. When things go wrong, we need someone to pay for it. To quench our thirst for justice, we seek closure—something or someone to free us from our collective guilt.

But there's a high cost to partaking in this game.

In the past, blame motivated the tragedy of human sacrifice, witch trials, lynchings, and the Holocaust. Today, it fuels war, ethnic cleansing, and hate crimes. It doesn't stop at the border of any country. It transcends every race, every religion, and every socio-economic class.

It's a psychological game of hot potato. We don't want to hold on when blame gets passed to us. So, we hand it off to others—creating the Blame Loop.

Beauty and the Beast

Sure, you say, blame is found in old Bible stories. But society has evolved since then, right? Unfortunately, no. Blame permeates our contemporary tales too.

There may not be any storyteller in the modern era more widely beloved than Walt Disney. The classic works of Disney conjure up nostalgic memories of idealized melodramas and utopian dreams. But many of these fables hold a dark message. According to the authors of *Ahead of the Lawmen: Law and Morality in Disney Animated Films*:

> *Often, the Disney-protagonist in some way punishes the villain for his/her actions in a way that exceeds what most Americans would consider the 'moral' response. However, when it suits the protagonist to do something that is immoral, no legal response is issued. In both cases, the protagonist is portrayed as being in the right and the outcome, therefore, is suitable and just.*

Many stories we tell revolve around a simplistic conclusion. Good things happen to good people. Bad things happen to bad people.

We tell these fables to our children to encourage good behavior. But, ironically, we're creating an inverse correlation at the same time. If something bad happens to me, I must be a bad person. I am blameworthy.

This mentality emphasizes assigning blame instead of learning lessons. Rather than finding flaws in our processes or information, we focus on who's at fault.

In the opening of Disney's animated feature, *Beauty and the Beast*, the young prince acts selfishly, so he is cursed to become a beast—a bad thing happens to a bad person. Later, when he acts selflessly, the love of his life—Belle—sees his inner beauty. A good thing happens to a good person. Then, the villain Gaston attempts to thwart the couple's budding romance. But he's defeated in the end—a bad thing happens to a bad person.

It's an ethical karma of sorts. Each time something bad happens, someone is to blame. Cause-and-effect.

Of course, reality is more complex than a Disney animation. In the workplace, outcomes don't always correspond to intent, effort, or even intelligence.

When a project fails—instead of immediately wondering who did something wrong—what if we asked: What assumptions did we make? Did we miss a step in our process? Would a different tool or approach have resulted in a better outcome?

By asking questions like this, how much more would we—or our team—learn to be more successful next time? How much could we grow together? How would that change our culture?

People who blame others don't necessarily realize they're doing something harmful. Instead they believe they are holding others accountable. It seems like the responsible thing to do. In a personal relationship, it may be characterized as tough love. At work, it's considered doing your job.

There's nothing wrong with wanting to know when something went wrong. By investigating the reason poor outcomes occurred, we can correct faulty assumptions or identify better decision criteria.

But the Blame Loop focuses on who did something wrong. It makes people the issue. Instead of learning from errors in the process—and making continuous improvements—personal blame inevitably leads to punishment, demotion, or termination. Of course, depending on the situation, disciplinary measures are sometimes necessary. But when an organization is caught in the Blame Loop, these tactics are the primary correction method.

A reliance on negative feedback leads to a toxic work culture where people constantly fear losing their job. Instead of increased productivity, people contract into a cover-your-ass mentality. This inhibits the creativity and innovation necessary to survive in the ever-changing landscape of today's marketplace.

One of the reasons we allow blame to run rampant is that we confuse it with the attributes of a healthy culture. Maybe some clarity is in order. Let's address that next.

Misunderstanding blame

We often use the word blame too broadly.

Right away, I want to clarify what I am addressing in this book. There are two primary forms of blame: causal and interpersonal.

Causal blame is blaming someone or something for inciting a negative event. Interpersonal blame is a reaction to an adverse event that attributes wrongdoing to a person's flawed character.

For example, a server at a restaurant spills a cold glass of water on a customer. Causal blame may focus on the condensation on the glass or an imbalanced serving tray leading to the water spilling.

Interpersonal blame focuses on whether the server intended to spill the water. Maybe the customer complained about waiting too long for drinks and felt the server spilled on them as retribution. Interpersonal blame could also condemn the server because he or she is inept at their job. Essentially, one is looking for a personal flaw, not simply cause and effect.

Let's take a look at another example.

When you miss the start of your child's school play, you blame your spouse for leaving work late. The story you tell yourself is that you're objective; you're only identifying about impersonal causes.

But, in reality—because you both missed your child's first scene on stage—you're blaming your spouse for not caring enough about your child's feelings. You assume he or she are more dedicated to work than to family events. Your anger or resentment is based on a judgment of their character. It's very personal.

I address causal and interpersonal blame but focus more on the latter. This is because interpersonal blame is more prevalent and, by far, the most damaging.

When you hold someone at fault, whether it's yourself or someone else, blame festers and transforms into resentment. This bitterness doesn't serve justice or fairness. Instead, it seeks to unleash the tension created by wrongdoing. It's a form of revenge.

'Guilt' can be two different things. It's the feeling you have when you know you did something wrong—an internal experience.

But guilt can also mean judgment, potentially in the legal sense, that someone has committed an error or much worse. A jury can find someone guilty of committing a crime.

I believe that guilt is adaptive and helpful—it's holding something we've done, or failed to do, up against our values and feeling psychological discomfort.

Brené Brown

The next word, 'responsibility,' means that you own the consequences of your actions. Responsibility has much better boundaries than self-blame because we don't take ownership of another person's actions. Similarly, 'accountability' is accepting the consequences of future actions.

Hanna Pickard, professor of philosophy and bioethics at Johns Hopkins University, argues that blame can be irrational. According to her analysis "Irrational Blame," when we say another person is to blame, we mean one of three things:

1. They are blameworthy.
2. We should blame them.
3. We do blame them.

Pickard describes these as three distinct propositions. In other words, we decide on them independently of one another. Even if we don't honestly believe someone is blameworthy, we may decide it's in our interest to blame them. Of course, then we have to decide whether or not actually to blame them.

This may seem trivial, but it shows we can blame someone after deciding we shouldn't—all the while acknowledging they aren't blameworthy.

Now you see how blame can be irrational. We can choose to blame someone without any reason whatsoever. We just feel like it. We hold onto resentment, even when it is not warranted.

When my business partner and I started our ad agency in 2006, we positioned ourselves as a boutique shop. We were a small, agile team without the bloated salaries and pricey office space of a more prominent firm. Customers appreciated that they were getting a fair rate for our services and that we could quickly adjust to meet their needs. They liked our low overhead.

Blame is a type of corporate bloat. It's emotional overhead that gets added to every interaction after a mistake or failure.

A culture of blame has a similar effect as other kinds of overhead. It takes a tax on organizations—creating fear and eroding trust. Team members sense that they don't have the support to make suggestions or the freedom to propose new ideas.

As a result, your company requires more effort and expanded timelines to take on new initiatives. These delays and difficulties translate, on the balance sheet, into financial overhead.

One of the pioneers of organizational psychology, Edgar Schein, emphasized the importance of psychological safety. He encouraged leaders to create a work atmosphere where employees understood it was safe to take interpersonal risks. Schein found this eliminated the anxiety that made it difficult for learning and change to occur.

The emotional overhead of blame undermines a person's sense of psychological safety in the workplace. How can you feel safe when expecting others will pin failures and mistakes on you? If you see a track record of leaders punishing scapegoats without understanding the root cause of a problem, you'll feel anxious about taking any risk yourself.

Yet if blame is irrational and counterproductive, why do we use it so much?

Unfortunately, we have many reasons for choosing it.

Blame is a defense mechanism. When something bad happens, blame gives us an idea of what to do next. It's related to our fight or flight mechanism. We blame others as a fight response and often blame ourselves as a way to take flight—rather than dealing maturely with a situation.

Hypnotically, blame feels like an actual answer. We humans are pattern-recognition machines. This helped us identify predators in the savannah. But in our cubicles, the everyday patterns we see can involve skewed perspectives and inherent biases. When there's a void of information—not knowing why an adverse event occurred—we take the easy road and blame. We resent someone for something they did not actually do

It's more than a bad habit; it has devastating effects.

An agency of blame

In the '90s, advertising was going through a transformation.

Ad campaigns were created on computers, but much of the media was still traditional. In the first agency I worked at, we developed national campaigns that were seen in newspapers and magazines, as well as on TV and billboards. In a short time, I worked my way up to art director and then creative director in charge of ideas and production.

My team was developing on a catalog for a client, a relatively large project. The designer had created the multipage computer document and prepared it for the printer. His file was converted into four-color separation film. Each page had negatives for each color to be printed: cyan, magenta, yellow, and black. The catalog was dozens of pages, so hundreds of sheets of film were produced.

Before the printer used the films to etch printing plates for the entire catalog, the printer sent us a blue-line proof to check for any last-minute errors. Once I received it, I realized we had a big problem. Every single page number was incorrect. My team needed to resubmit a new file, and the printer would have to recreate the film for every page.

When I explained this to my boss, the agency's owner, she told me to blame the printer. "Tell them to redo the film for free," she said without a hint of shame.

The mistake was not the printer's fault. We knew it. The printer knew it as well. Our graphic designer had made the error in-house—both the art director and I missed it when we approved their work.

My boss wouldn't hear of it.

"Tell them to redo it for free," she insisted.

I refused—a heated argument ensued.

I was willing to take responsibility for the mistake. The graphic designer made the error, but it was my job to ensure whatever left our department was ready to print. I expected the cost of new film would be taken out of my paycheck. I was willing to be the scapegoat to that extent. But I didn't anticipate the actual consequences.

I called the printer and asked them to only print the page numbers on the black plate instead of 'registration black'—which uses every color. The difference wouldn't be noticeable on something as small as page numbers. This meant only one out of every four sets of film would need to be redone. Additionally, I asked if they could discount the film, which they did. This reduced the cost but, ultimately, our agency would pay for the mistake. I spent the weekend metaphorically kicking myself.

On Monday morning, I showed up at my usual time and parked behind the office. I unlocked the back door and saw the owner sitting at my desk in my chair. She smiled and announced, "You're fired."

I was caught off-guard. "You mean because I didn't make the printer redo the film for free?"

"Yes," she said flatly.

I stood like a deer caught in headlights. Then I thought about the process of finding another job. I realized years of my work was still on the agency computer.

"OK. I just need to gather a few things."

She handed me a box. "Here are your things."

She had thought this through, and I was unprepared.

I blinked, "I need to copy a few files from my computer."

"That's my computer, and you won't go near it."

"But..."

"Leave!"

I walked back out to my car with my cardboard box of personal items and a bewildered look on my face. What just happened?

I carried the baggage of being fired with me for years. It damaged my confidence and fractured my trust in leadership.

Destroying relationships

"If we don't trust one another, then we aren't going to engage in open, constructive, ideological conflict. And we'll just continue to preserve a sense of artificial harmony."

Patrick Lencioni, *The Five Dysfunctions of a Team*

Many leaders think they have a great corporate culture, but it often boils down to a belief that everyone gets along with each other. It's more likely that what we call 'getting along' is actually the artificial harmony mentioned by Lencioni.

People act nice to each other but don't trust each other. Since they don't trust, they're not honest. They're not genuine because they want to avoid conflict—even constructive conflict.

I experienced this in a corporate role with a professional services firm years ago. When I joined, they bragged about the culture. They were proud of how everyone was remarkably nice to each other. This wasn't common in the industry.

At first blush, this environment appealed to me. Then I learned more. I realized that people readily agreed with each other while in meetings but later did whatever they wanted behind closed doors.

When expectations weren't met, finding people who truly could cooperate was challenging. For his part, the CEO didn't hold individuals accountable as long as they were getting results.

When the lack of teamwork caused other areas of the company to suffer. Department heads were blamed, chastised, and sometimes fired. This created an underlying tension that wasn't obvious to the casual observer. It was like black mold—hidden from plain sight but killing those who unknowingly lived with it.

Healthy teamwork was sacrificed to avoid conflict. Blame was the result.

Remember how I said that blame is like playing hot potato? Part of the reason we revert to a children's game is that we don't manage conflict well. We're desperate to assign blame elsewhere to avoid being the one stuck with it.

If you ever played hot potato as a kid, you remember the anxiety of holding the potato and trying to pass it off without dropping it. The stakes feel more significant when the 'potato' is blame for something that has failed—like a project, business, or relationship.

During this emotional upheaval, we have difficulty identifying reality versus the emotions gripping us. We struggle to discern what happened as opposed to what we felt. We can often blame others for something that didn't even occur.

The harder you need to be on the problem, usually the softer you need to be on the people, if the people—their emotions, their egos, and so on—are not going to get in the way of solving the problem.

William Ury, *Getting to Yes*

Emotional upheaval isn't the only consequence of blame.

Recently, the Society for Human Resource Management calculated the cost of turnover created by toxic workplace culture. The total tabulation was $223 billion! That is roughly the entire GDP of Greece.

Since blame is a significant contributor to a toxic culture, it is a crucial factor in this staggering financial impact.

Meanwhile, even the workers who don't quit can be affected by a blame-saturated workplace. For years studies have shown that roughly one-third of the global workforce is actively disengaged from their organization's goals and productivity. Another third are partially disengaged. That's two-thirds of workers who are not fully engaged with their work.

What is the number one factor in employee engagement?

Positive motivation.

The opposite of positive motivation is negative motivation. When employees feel blamed, they can become resentful and disengaged. These feelings can be so toxic that they can lead to anxiety and depression.

The stress caused by blame can lead to physical illness, resulting in rising healthcare costs and absenteeism. All of this emotional upheaval costs organizations, and their employees, dearly in both morale and dollars.

When it comes to employee engagement, blame is clearly an enemy. Engaging with this aspect of workplace culture is not simply a 'warm fuzzy.' It affects the bottom line.

To improve employee engagement, it's essential to reduce the amount of blame. By doing this, organizations can create a more positive workplace culture that nurtures true engagement.

Blame destroys trust

Blame makes it hard to place our trust in others.

This happened to me after I was unceremoniously fired from the design firm. I lost my sense of security with the person blaming me. But, on the other side, we also lose confidence in those we condemn. It goes both ways. Blame makes it hard to create any psychological safety in teams and organizations.

This doesn't happen as an isolated incident, though. Erosion of trust is part of a related sequence of events.

Blame lowers trust.

Lower trust creates interpersonal conflict.

Interpersonal conflict increases blame.

And the vicious cycle continues.

This cycle devastates our ability to collaborate, so we rely on independence instead. Our workplaces become collections of self-serving individuals working toward their own agenda. The driving motivator is WIIFM. What's In It For Me?

It's no wonder today's work cultures are notoriously toxic.

Meanwhile, while some leaders allows this cycle to endure via blissful ignorance, others actually promote it—seeing it as a net positive (a corporate survival of the fittest).

Employees are rewarded for seeking out individual recognition and achievement. Owning and admitting mistakes can affect your performance marks, compensation, and job security. In most workplaces, it's safer to blame others than to accept responsibility.

There's a story that during the Industrial Era, migrant workers lived in apartments with thin walls and noisy floors. While going to bed, they sometimes heard the tenant directly above removing a shoe and dropping it to the floor after an exhausting day of work. For the worker in the lower flat, the next few moments were spent waiting for the other shoe to drop.

When failure occurs in a blame culture, employees often feel anxious—anticipating how leadership will react. The other shoe drops when someone is blamed. This dynamic creates a workplace where those hoping to survive throw others under the bus.

You can't cultivate trust in your workplace if those on your team are uncertain about survival.

The result is a toxic workplace culture where everyone is looking out for themselves, and no one is thinking about the team's best interests. No wonder so many workers are disengaged and unhappy.

When we reduce blame, we increase trust.

When we increase trust, we reduce interpersonal conflict.

When we reduce interpersonal conflict, we minimize blame.

And the positive cycle continues.

The second arrow

According to the legend, the Buddha once asked a student, "If an arrow strikes a person, is it painful?"

The student replied, "It is."

The Buddha then asked, "If a second arrow strikes the person, is that even more painful?"

The student replied again, "It is."

The Buddha explained, "In life, we cannot always control the first arrow. However, the second arrow is our reaction to the first. And with this second arrow comes the possibility of choice."

In relationships, the second arrow can be many things. Sometimes it's blame striking someone already experiencing the pain of failure. By firing a second arrow, we add guilt to the situation.

Of course, I'm not suggesting that people shouldn't experience the consequences of their choices. We need that to learn. But they can suffer those consequences—and learn from their mistakes—without the shame of a second arrow.

When we remove blame from the equation, we open up the possibility for growth. We create an environment where people can feel safe to experiment, take risks, and innovate. And when people feel safe, they're more likely to be engaged and motivated.

The next time you're tempted to blame someone for a mistake, ask yourself if firing the second arrow is really in the best interests of your team. In most cases, it simply compounds problems and makes it more difficult to find a solution.

When we catch ourselves reaching for the second arrow, we can make a different choice. We can choose to lead with empathy and compassion. And when we do, we might find that the person on the receiving end responds in kind.

The little girl who changed Charles Barkley's life

The blame game is the core pattern of almost every destructive conflict I have ever witnessed. The costs of the blame game are huge. It escalates disputes. It prevents us from resolving them. It undermines our power.

William Ury, *Getting To Yes With Yourself*

For sixteen memorable seasons, basketball legend Charles Barkley racked up accomplishments. He was an 11-time NBA All-Star, the league's Most Valuable Player, and twice a member of the USA Olympic team. As a power forward, Barkley is one of the top 20 career rebounders, despite being below-average height for the NBA. Even though he never won an NBA championship, his career was a major success. He parlayed his popularity into an admirable second career as a sports analyst on TNT.

But Barkley was widely criticized for an incident early in his professional basketball career. And his response changed his life.

In 1991, a fan in the stands shouted racial slurs at him. Still in his 20s, Barkley lost his composure and walked over to the baseline behind the goal. He spat in the direction of the verbally abusive fan. Unfortunately, his spit landed on a little girl seated nearby.

In an interview on *In Depth with Graham Bensinger*, Barkley shared how this became a watershed moment for him. "I was sitting in a hotel room, and I was like, 'Dude, what the hell is wrong with you? What are you so angry about?'"

He identified that much of his anger came from blaming others for his choices and actions. He took ownership of his responsibilities instead of holding onto that negativity.

"From that day forward, every time I played basketball, I said, 'Just let people see your talent. You don't have to be mad at anybody else.' And so that was the turn around for me."

Barkley didn't stop at changing his on-court attitude. He took responsibility for the spitting incident as well. The future NBA Hall of Famer reached out to the family of the young girl. He offered them tickets to future games and developed a friendship with them.

You could make a long list of public figures who didn't turn around as Barkley did. Instead, they continued down a path of self-destructive behavior fed by the anger of blaming others and refusing to take personal responsibility.

> *Anger is an acid that can do more harm to the vessel in which it is stored than to anything on which it is poured.*
>
> Mark Twain

Or, as author Susan Cheever shared, this resentment toward others "is like taking poison and waiting for the other person to die."

It's time to own your responsibility and put the poison down.

Failing vs. Falling

The captivating author and speaker Simon Sinek recently shared his frustrations with the topic of broad categorization. We use the same word for mild and easily treatable melanoma as we do for small cell carcinomas with a 93% fatality rate—both are called 'cancer.'

Then Sinek expanded this realization to a concept we'll discuss a lot: 'failure.' He said, "Failure could be absolutely catastrophic, or it could be a minor hiccup, but the problem is we call it failure. So I think we need to use different terms."

Think about falling down; it happens naturally and frequently. And that usually means we must pick ourselves back up. Yet, Sinek suggests, if every fall feels like a failure, we'll simply lie there and complain instead of taking risks and pushing boundaries.

When we communicate to our team that failure is like fatal cancer, we also create a culture where boundaries are never pushed. People play it safe. They actively steer clear of the promising new ideas that await across that boundary in untrampled territory.

The liminal space at the border of what we've done before is where new things are discovered, experimented with, and proven or disproven. If we never enter that space, we continue to repeat the same old ideas while our competitors in the market find innovative ways to serve their customers (and, soon, maybe our customers).

Sinek continued, "We have to give people the opportunity to fall and let them either learn to fix their own problems or guide them."

Then he reminisced about his mentor, Peter Intermaggio, a boss from years ago who would never directly answer a question. When Sinek queried him about the next steps in a process, Peter would reply cryptically, "What do you think we should do?"

"My god. If I knew, I wouldn't be asking."

"Well, what do you think?" Peter insisted.

"I think we should do this."

"Then do that."

Sinek didn't always do the right thing. Sometimes he'd screw up, and Intermaggio would ask, "Now, what are you going to do?"

But Sinek never worried about being fired because of screwing up. He knew his learning process was held in a respectful, objective manner by his boss. Now, Sinek sees the value and wisdom in this approach to 'falling.'

I love this story. It highlights how the term failure can cause us to identify with our setbacks. If you're a runner, you'll probably fall down one day. You won't suddenly identify as a 'faller.' You're just a runner who fell.

We should react similarly when we, or others, fail at something. Identifying with failure is another way of blaming, giving it a hook. It's interpersonal blame, not causal. And it isn't productive because it often ignores the actual cause, distracting us from finding a solution.

Missing the mark

Imagine an archer standing in a sunny field with a bow. She aims toward a distant bullseye. She releases the shaft and it arcs gracefully across the grass, but falls short of the target she was aiming for.

What is your first thought? Do you assume she was trying to miss the mark? Do you criticize her motivation? Do you blame her for the misfire?

In all likelihood, you probably believe she tried her best. If it's someone you know, you might encourage her to take another shot.

Too often, we use interpersonal blame to pin the failure on individuals. We feel someone must've been negligent, incompetent, or purposefully malicious. We've been doing this for millennia. We even have a word for it.

'Sinner' is a loaded term that seems to convey someone was willfully defiant or just plain evil. When you look closer, though, it is more nuanced.

In the ancient Greek of the New Testament, *hamartia* is a word used to describe sin. It's actually a term from archery and navigation, meaning 'to miss the mark' or 'go wide' of the target. In other words, the sin of *hamartia* implies that a person's action was an error, not willful defiance. This is the concept the writers of the New Testament were actually trying to convey before it became varnished over by centuries of church doctrine.

So should we be hell-bent (literally) on blaming others for their errors? Wouldn't it be healthier to help correct an archer's aim—or a traveler's path—instead of blaming them for going wide of their objective? If the goal is to hit our target, the answer is obvious.

When bad things happen to good people

We must sense that bad things don't characterize us or others. Think about the phrase, "When bad things happen to good people." In the 1980s, Rabbi Harold Kushner wrote a book by this title. In it, he told the story of a man who had survived the Holocaust and, in the aftermath, started a family—rebuilding his life.

"Life seemed good after the horrors of the concentration camp," Kushner wrote. But, suddenly, the man's family died in a forest fire. His friends were sure someone was culpable for the accident. They encouraged him to call for an investigation into the fire's origins.

Kushner continues, "An inquiry would set him against other people. Was someone negligent? Whose fault was it? Being against other people, setting out to find a villain, and accusing other people of being responsible for your misery, only makes a lonely person lonelier. Life, he concluded, has to be lived for something, not just against something."

When we focus on blame, we set ourselves against others, as Kushner phrases it. We look for villains. We stop growing. This is why some businesses stagnate. Their culture becomes steeped in blame instead of innovating to solve problems.

Not only does the Blame Loop create fear, but it inhibits people from taking risks. It turns our heads toward the past. Not in a helpful way, learning from our mistakes so we can improve in the future, but solely to fix blame on someone. We don't grow from this methodology. Instead, we try to shrink others around us—providing the illusion that we are growing. Pseudo-growth.

A perfect storm in Italy

Fifteen years ago—in the picturesque Italian city of Perugia—Meredith Kercher, a British college student, was found dead. The murder scene was grizzly, and the victim was a beautiful young woman with a radiant smile. It was shocking and tragic.

Less than a week after finding the body, Italian police identified their suspects—Kercher's American roommate, Amanda Knox, and Knox's boyfriend, Raffaele Sollecito. Without any physical evidence, Knox was convicted for Kercher's murder.

How did Amanda go from being an innocent, fun-loving college kid to a convicted murderer in the eyes of the public?

At the start of the investigation, authorities had little evidence to help them piece together how Meredith died. The victim had been stripped, possibly violently, since her bra clasp was broken off. Some of Kercher's bodily injuries were consistent with sexual assault, but the medical examiner stated the findings were not unequivocal. Indications pointed to there being more than one murderer. The chief investigator took this circumstantial evidence and formed a theory—the murder resulted from a sex game gone wrong.

Meanwhile, Amanda exhibited strange behavior near the time of the murder, like public displays of affection with her boyfriend. Her story about returning home from her boyfriend's place and finding Kercher's body the morning after the incident didn't make sense to the investigator either. She seemed unfazed by finding blood in the bathroom, even taking a shower before discovering other signs of an intruder later.

Pairing the evidence with Knox's behavior and illogical story, the prosecutor's theory evolved to include her and her boyfriend as participants in the crime.

The media, the prosecution, and even the police fixated on Amanda. They made her out to be a sex-crazed, drug-fueled party girl who had killed her roommate in a fit of jealousy.

It was an intoxicating narrative—perfect for the tabloids—that allowed everyone to forget that there was no physical evidence linking her to the murder. As messy as the scene was, there was none of Knox and Sollecito's DNA found in the room where Kercher died. There was no eyewitness testimony locating them at her apartment.

The prosecutor had one last piece of circumstantial evidence—a knife found at Knox and Sollecito's apartment with Kercher's DNA on the blade and Knox's DNA on the handle. It wasn't the murder weapon, but—because it was found in their apartment—the prosecutor argued it must have been used in some capacity.

With no apparent motive and no hard evidence, the prosecutor relied on a sensational narrative that clearly captivated the public. Authorities needed a suspect to blame. Unfortunately for Amanda, she was the perfect scapegoat.

Why? First, Amanda was a foreigner, so she was easier to blame. People are more willing to believe ill of an outsider.

Next, there was a lack of clarity. In the absence of evidence, authorities made assumptions and let guesswork lead them down the wrong path. The theory that Meredith was killed as part of an ill-fated sex game was flimsy.

Third, there was an appealing narrative. The press became infatuated with painting Knox as a femme fatale. This assertion made the story sensational—catnip for the media and the public.

Finally, we have confirmation bias. Even though the facts didn't back up the original theory regarding Knox, authorities ignored their lack of evidence and accepted only what supported their initial speculations.

The perfect storm of scapegoating factors led to Amanda Knox being arrested and convicted of killing her roommate. We'll revisit Amanda's story later. But, first, I want to share more of my personal journey with the consequences of succumbing to the Blame Loop.

Who's to blame when you're in charge?

After I was fired from my first agency job, I still yearned for the business. This time, however, I didn't want to work for an advertising firm. I wanted to own one.

For the next few years, I traded agency work for internal marketing roles in software and tech companies. All the while, though, I looked for partner opportunities in ad agencies.

When someone I knew needed a creative director to help her boutique ad agency, I scraped together money—and took out a loan—to become an equity partner. I was ecstatic. I had endless ideas of what we could do—an enormous vision for what the agency could become in the next few years.

Our niche was the residential real estate industry. Our clients included mortgage companies, builders, developers, and the area home builders association. In addition, I worked on two television programs focused on real estate.

The newly-invigorated agency started with a bang. We earned new clients. We won awards. Most importantly, our clients became more successful due, in part, to our efforts. I was in heaven.

Sadly, the dream lasted less than twenty-four months.

The Great Recession

The ecstasy of building the business led to the reality that our finances were stretched too thin. Our office space was too expensive. Payroll expanded as we added staff to handle new clientele. Our margins were incredibly narrow—leaving us little room to fail.

Then, just as we were in the middle of an aggressive growth phase, the Great Recession of 2008 hit.

As you probably remember, the financial crisis decimated the real estate industry in particular. Our little agency reeled.

We tried to recover, but clients were going out of business due to the implosion. The ones that survived cut their advertising and marketing budgets to the bone or brought those services in-house.

We were left vulnerable. Our risky investment into expanding became fruitless. After months of haggling with vendors, negotiating with clients, and meeting with advisors, we closed our doors.

At first, I quietly blamed my business partner for the death of our firm. She was the majority owner. She made decisions that I couldn't overrule. I was angry because I felt these (outside-of-my-control) choices caused the failure of our business.

Later, I blamed myself for not trusting my instincts and speaking up more. I felt it was my fault for not realizing we had too many clients in the formerly booming real estate market.

In reality, my partner and I shared responsibility for the failure. When I mention that the business closed its doors in 2008, most people nod sympathetically. They know how challenging the market was after the real estate bubble popped.

Honestly, even if we had diversified our clientele more, there's no guarantee our business would have survived. The Great Recession impacted the entire economy.

Still, closing up shop felt very personal to me. The experience left me feeling snake-bit. It hurt my self-confidence and my trust in others.

Shame and self-loathing lingered overhead like a stormy rain cloud over a cartoon character. At the same time, I blamed other people for the business failure. Bitterness grew inside me.

Moreover, I blamed outside circumstances I couldn't control. These made me feel that no matter how hard I worked or smart my decisions were, I'd still fail.

Yes, snake-bit seems like the perfect term. When someone is bit by a snake, there are dire consequences for not extracting the venom immediately. Unfortunately, those consequences were coming for me in ways I never imagined.

2

"*Forgiveness and mercy mean that, bit by bit,
you begin to outshine the resentment.*"

Anne Lamott, *Hallelujah Anyway*

Scapegoat Salvation

2

Arbitrary responses to unmet expectations

What happens when results don't live up to expectations?

The gap between expectations and reality creates interpersonal tension. It breaks up teams, friendships, business partnerships, and even marriages. We grapple with the challenge of reconciling the results we hoped for versus the results we ended up with.

There are countless books, webinars, and courses about setting goals, but we spend very little time addressing what happens when we miss those goals. Usually, it is one of two things:

1. There is hell to pay
2. Nothing

From the perspective of most employees, the reason leaders choose between these options often seems arbitrary and unclear. This is why many leaders appear to be mercurial to those who work for them. An employee's fate seems tied to a coin toss or something irrelevant, such as what their boss ate for lunch. Either way, they feel it's outside their control.

They may be right.

And there are few things scarier than knowing your life is in the hands of someone over whom you have little, if any, influence. Let me share a story about one such boss.

A friend of mine was working for a local dentist who was utterly unpredictable. She would chide an employee for gossiping one day but then join in on a similar character assassination—with gusto—the very next day. The dentist would make decisions on hiring, promotions, and raises based on arbitrary criteria, to the point that everyone knew she played favorites.

My friend found herself wanting to keep her head down and avoid making any waves. It was easier to maintain the status quo than not knowing if the additional effort would reap a dramatically positive or negative outcome.

It seemed like the boss had one employee who was her favorite. Not because the woman performed well at work but for her spirited personality. On more than one occasion, when the boss's pet didn't like someone, their remaining employment was short.

But even this person lost favor when she made a wisecrack and offended the dentist, who previously would revel in these friendly jabs from her favorite. The joke soured their relationship, resulting in the sidekick getting booted from the dental office.

After this, the office culture was full of anxiety, confusion, and distrust. My friend and her colleagues found new employment elsewhere as they sought a more stable, healthy work environment—someplace where their livelihood didn't rest in the hands of a boss who seemed wholly indifferent to their welfare.

This cycle continues everywhere. Instead of proposing a better alternative, we attribute this toxic behavior to the nature of business. Competitors are nipping at our heels, and we don't have the luxury of even pretending to care for employees. It's a fight for survival.

Many leaders don't grasp the nuance of responsibility versus blame. They believe attributing blame to someone will improve that person's performance in the future. Instead, it creates tension as employees recognize leadership will continue to find a scapegoat. And, next time, it might be them.

The Blame Loop amplifies stress because it doesn't correlate to individual performance but to factors outside his or her control. The workforce feels powerless to shape their own future. And when something unexpected happens, everyone waits with anxiety for the other shoe to fall.

Eventually, some employees leave these harmful environments. Unfortunately, they carry the trauma they experienced with them. They may find a new job that sounds better but still have difficulty trusting their colleagues and leadership.

At the new place, they hear the same promises and clichés from executives. They see the same goal-setting behavior from managers. They hear the same worries and concerns from coworkers.

Maybe everything isn't the same. Perhaps the new company's purpose statement sounds more authentic. Still, it could all be lip service unless these principles are backed up with action.

This is why company culture is so influential. It needs to be more than words. Culture is the collective, observable patterns of a group. What is the team's habit when something goes wrong? Do they blame and scapegoat, or do they make a sober assessment of what transpired?

Some people may feel their entire professional life is spent working for an angry god who needs human sacrifice to appease his vengeance. Isn't that where the concept of a scapegoat originated?

The original scapegoat

Aaron awoke with the death of two of his sons fresh on his mind. They had been burned alive. They were careless with fire, and the consequences were fatal. On this morning, Aaron would be risking the same fate. He would be in the same place his sons were when they died. He would be lighting a similar flame.

He resolved in his mind that he would not be careless because this was no ordinary fire. It was part of a precise ritual necessary to approach God.

I'm pausing here to acknowledge that I'm again introducing a Bible story into a business book. I realize not every reader is familiar with or appreciative of these stories. All I ask is that you bear with me, as this account will give context to some central concepts we'll be discussing as we go forward. It doesn't require you to convert or believe anything different.

Okay. Back to Aaron.

Aaron was the high priest for the nation of Israel. He was the right-hand man for his brother Moses. Yes, this is the same Moses portrayed by Charlton Heston in *The Ten Commandments*. While the 1956 classic film focuses on visually-spectacular scenes—such as the Israelites crossing the Red Sea (which God had miraculously parted), and Moses receiving two tablets on Mount Sinai—it does not show how the ancient law was fulfilled.

At the center of the nation of Israel was the Tabernacle—a giant, portable tent they broke down and rebuilt as they moved camp. They were wandering a desert where enemies could attack at any time, so ease-of-transport was paramount to their collective survival.

Aaron and his sons were the first priests of Israel. Their duties included entering the Holy of Holies—a small, sacred space where the Ark of the Covenant resided within the Tabernacle. According to tradition, this was where the presence of God dwelled among His people. So, the rules and rituals for entering such a revered place were exact. Aaron's sons, Nadab and Abihu, disregarded these strict guidelines. They offered an unauthorized fire in the presence of the Ark, and a greater fire from God consumed them both.

It was a horrific sight for their father to witness. Yet, Aaron was silent. Moses ordered Aaron's nephews to remove the bodies of their cousins. He then instructed Aaron and his remaining two sons not to follow the custom of tearing their clothes in mourning. They had to stay in the Tabernacle, or they would die as well.

These were high stakes—the highest.

Moses, Aaron, and all the Israelites had come out of Egypt, a land where the gods were fickle. After leaving Egypt, the law gave the Israelites guidance; it assured them. Their God was not inconsistent. He not only enforced the law; He abided by it. He could be trusted. Trust. At the time, this was a new idea in society.

After Aaron's sons died, Moses instructed Aaron how they would proceed. He asked them to observe The Day of Atonement, when all the nation's sins are reconciled with God.

Once again, the ritual was detailed. Aaron had to perform sacrificial offerings to cleanse himself to enter the Holy of Holies. Then he needed to sacrifice a goat, one chosen to bear the sins of all the people of Israel. A red cord was placed around the goat's neck; then, it was led away from the community into the wilderness.

This is the origin of the scapegoat.

The Hebrew name for the desolate place the scapegoat was sent is *Azazel*. There are many discussions about what this name means, but it sounds like 'Oz-oz-elle.' So, we'll call him Ozzie.

Poor Ozzie didn't do anything wrong. In fact, his fate was chosen through chance. The men cast lots to select Ozzie. This lousy roll of the dice meant all the blame was placed on the goat's head, and he was expelled. Almost certain death awaited in the wilderness.

Day of Atonement is a ritual for resetting society. Over the year, things would get out of whack because people and relationships tend to be messy. We hurt others, intentionally or unintentionally. We perceive others are hurting us, even if they don't intend it. For the practitioners of Judaism, Day of Atonement acts as a do-over, a fresh start when all miscommunication is dialed back to zero.

Alright. That was a lot of Bible story. You might wonder why I unloaded it on you. What does this have to do with business?

Let's unpack it a bit.

We have a tribe of people wandering in a desert. They face death and uncertainty every day. Other tribes fight them, take their stuff, and possibly kill them. This creates tension, which likely finds its way into their culture and creates interpersonal conflict. People hurt each other in myriad ways, and those people retaliate. The tension escalates as they blame each other more and more.

This is where the scapegoat comes in. By taking the blame and removing it from society, the goat diffuses the blame bomb. The slate is wiped clean.

So back to business.

To my mind, companies are modern-day tribes. Together a corporate team fights for financial survival against other tribes (which we call 'competitors').

This creates tension that can lead to interpersonal conflict.

Conflict tends to escalate as blame is tossed back and forth like a grenade ready to explode. The spiral continues until a scapegoat is saddled with the blame to diffuse the situation.

Employees come with baggage from other jobs (like the Israelites had from their time spent in Egypt). It can be hard to trust the boss when people seem to be terminated randomly for things outside their control.

Leaders must be intentional about establishing a strong culture; otherwise, today's Moses seems no better than last year's Pharaoh.

We could use a reset button, but we can't do a ritual with a goat in the workplace.

The white knight vs. the dark night

In the Christopher Nolan-directed movie, *The Dark Knight*, Harvey Dent is the district attorney for the fictional city of Gotham. He's been cleaning up a metropolitan area overrun with crime as he fearlessly puts mob bosses behind bars. In a city full of corruption, he is a saint. Blameless.

Harvey is an even bigger hero than Batman because he doesn't hide behind a mask. He isn't a vigilante. The D.A. does everything by the book. Later, he falls victim to an explosion that kills his fiancé, Rachel, and leaves him deformed. Tragically, this incident tips him over the edge psychologically. With the evil prodding of Batman's nemesis, the Joker, Harvey transforms into the villainous persona Two-Face and goes on a killing spree.

As Two-Face, Dent doles out vengeance upon those he holds responsible for the death of Rachel. He flips a coin to decide whether or not to punish each perpetrator. Heads, you go free. Tails, death.

Two-Face starts with criminals but eventually goes after the chief of police, Commissioner Gordon, who is with his wife and son. Unbeknownst to Gordon, his men had secretly abducted Rachel, which led to her death. The commissioner isn't perfect, but he isn't responsible for the tragedy. So Batman intervenes.

He convinces Two-Face that all three men (Commissioner Gordon, Batman, and Harvey Dent) are equally responsible for not saving Rachel.

Unconvinced, Two-Face is ready to deliver justice. He points his gun at Batman, "You first." Two-Face flips a coin. Tails. Bang! He shoots Batman, who crumples and falls, clutching his stomach.

Two-Face then holds the gun to his own head. Gripped by regret and self-loathing, he flips a coin. Heads, go free. The D.A.-turned-criminal actually looks disappointed.

Finally, Two-Face aims at Commissioner Gordon's son. "Your turn, Gordon."

"You're right, Harvey," Gordon says. "Rachel's death was all my fault. Punish me—"

"I'm about to," Two-Face replies. "Tell your boy it's going to be alright. Lie. Like I lied." (Referring to how, while still Harvey Dent, he told Rachel everything would be okay before she died.)

Gordon's pain-ridden eyes lock with his son's. He obediently stammers, "It's going to be alright, son."

Two-Face flips the coin in the air. As it turns slowly, Batman—wounded but not dead—throws himself into Two-Face, knocking the internally-conflicted man off a high platform to his death.

Gordon checks on the injured Batman, who explains he will take the blame for the heinous things Harvey/Two-Face did. Only they know the truth. It's the only way to maintain Harvey Dent as a 'white knight' hero for the community. People will continue to believe in the good they saw in Dent. The city will avoid falling into chaos. As a result, Batman will be the 'dark knight.'

The Joker perverted Dent, the city's savior, to prove anyone could be corrupted. He was right. However, the clown-faced villain didn't count on someone else absorbing that blame instead of letting it land on Harvey. The Joker never imagined that any person would choose to be a scapegoat.

To take the blame.

To be hated and cast out.

If we're honest, we wouldn't expect that either. We expect most people to be selfish and point the blame elsewhere. We see otherwise decent leaders do something as arbitrary as flipping a coin to decide who should be the scapegoat.

Meanwhile, the storyline of this popular film taps into society's need for a scapegoat. When bad things happen, we feel helpless. Justice and morality are casualties in a ruthless world. We don't feel we have control over political unrest, the threat of nuclear war, climate issues, economic instability, or global pandemics.

We think we need a hero, but it seems like things are spiraling out of control. No one is capable or trustworthy enough for the task. In the end, we want to do something with the blame.

Thus, as a result of several millennia of scapegoating, we're very good at assigning blame to the wrong individuals.

Are scapegoats necessary?

Scapegoating is a common practice. So much so that it may make you wonder if it's just a necessary part of life.

Renowned historian and philosopher René Girard proposed that scapegoats were a key component for ancient civilizations as they evolved without an objectively fair justice system. At the time, it seems, scapegoats served a purpose.

Moreover, Girard argued that humans have an innate impulse for aggression. Because of this, conflict inevitably arises within a culture. It escalates as opposing factions seek revenge against each other. In response to this—across practically every ancient society and religion—ritual sacrifice provided a means for regaining harmony within a community.

The practice seems barbaric today, but it allowed a tribe to consolidate the escalating violence into one individual. This ritual acted as a relief valve and prevented group-wide violence from destroying society. Interestingly, in modern times, we see similar occurrences within the workplace.

While large companies may have corporate guidelines to shield the firm from liability, they often lack any sense of justice. Employees often don't feel the H.R. department is entirely objective since they serve the company and report to leadership—who may be that employee's antagonist on a specific issue.

Additionally, team members may be concerned that pursuing justice would jeopardize their job security. Choosing to seek external justice through the courts can be even riskier, leading to losing a job—opening them up to countersuits and protracted court battles where the company's deeper pockets win out.

As with ancient societies, aggression often escalates within modern organizations. Without an objective justice system, we look for other remedies. By placing blame on a scapegoat, we find a sense of personal relief while removing some elements of conflict from the group. Unfortunately, this results in unfairly blaming individuals, leaving those at fault without accountability for their roles.

And, in the same way that ancient civilizations relied on regular sacrifices, we often resort to scapegoating individuals on an ongoing basis. It's a vicious cycle that can tear apart a team.

When things go wrong, some leaders may point the finger of blame at their subordinates instead of addressing the issue. By doing so, they shift the focus away from their shortcomings.

Alternatively, individuals may be scapegoated for hostility towards the change when an organization alters its mission.

While in times of upheaval, it may be understandable for groups to seek stability. Scapegoating is short-sighted and harmful. It does nothing to help teams embrace change or solve instability. In fact, it often incites more chaos.

Scapegoating can damage team morale, resulting in the loss of the individual unfairly blamed. It incentivizes people to stay quiet about legitimate issues as they fear sharing too much will invite them to be blamed instead—the cycle of scapegoating continues as long as the underlying causes remain unaddressed.

Even though scapegoating serves a purpose, it's a poor tool. It does more damage to our workplace than it fixes. It's like killing a fly with an elephant gun. Sure, it gets the job done, but it creates way more collateral damage.

The shame of Oedipus

Let's look at the evolution of the scapegoat over time.

First, when ancient societies needed someone to blame, they often resorted to physical violence against that person. Then, as we have seen, this practice adapted into physical violence against animals—literal scapegoats.

Now, in modern society, the habit of scapegoating inflicts emotional damage upon people. We heap shame and guilt upon individuals to purge it from the group. We damage a single person's career, relationships, and financial stability to relieve the collective pressure caused by any failure.

One of the issues with scapegoating is it typically doesn't work if everyone recognizes the individual is innocent. To be effective, scapegoats must actually be guilty of something.

Returning to the work of René Girard, he used Oedipus as an example. The mythical Greek hero was an acceptable scapegoat since he had killed his father, the king, and married his mother. The citizens of Thebes saw his expulsion as a remedy for the plague ravaging their city. They wouldn't have accepted an innocent man as the one to bear their collective spite. But holding a morally corrupt person accountable gives a sense of purging their shame.

Too bad that modern life is not as clear-cut as it was for the citizens of Thebes. Today, in both our professional and personal life, the responsibility for a failure is often shared. Blaming an individual for group failure is a futile attempt to avoid shared responsibility. We're simply looking for a place to heap the guilt. But, in our hearts, we know it's wrong. We realize that another person doesn't deserve the emotional burden of the entire group.

What if, like ancient societies, we progress beyond using people as scapegoats? Instead of a living animal, we can choose to unload our emotional baggage upon an inanimate object.

On the front cover, I said you can blame this book. But you can put the blame anywhere you like. You decide where you put your psychological load. Maybe it's a plush toy shaped like a goat or a plastic figurine on your desk. You choose.

I should note that using an object as a scapegoat doesn't mean people are not held responsible for their actions. It doesn't mean you let someone continue to treat you or others poorly. There are consequences for people who hurt other people.

Remember how we discussed the difference between blame, responsibility, and accountability? There's never an excuse for abuse or bullying. Neither is this a justification for poor performance. Employees and leaders should be held to objective standards.

But using people as scapegoats is the absence of objectivity. In fact, it's the opposite of justice. Since this is so, one way to avoid unhealthy scapegoating is to seek fairness first.

Poison Control

If resentment is poison, I should have called Poison Control after our ad agency folded. I fell into a dangerous spiral when my unresolved feelings went unnoticed.

Unknowingly, I had stepped into a snake pit. And even a tiny snake can unleash deadly venom. The anger and guilt found their way into me and gradually coursed through my entire body. I held onto resentment toward others. I wallowed in the shame of failure.

I spent over a year trying to dig out of the financial hole I'd created for my family because of my failure. I had business-related loans to pay off. Meanwhile, my income had been cut in half because of the recession.

We couldn't afford quality health insurance during this time, and my five-year-old son broke his arm. Suddenly, in addition to the business debt, we had thousands of dollars in medical bills we couldn't pay. This fact led to bill collectors calling at all hours to ask for money we didn't have.

Whenever something bad happened, I didn't have the capacity to handle it.

The rainy day fund was long gone.

We couldn't repair our car after an accident.

We couldn't pay off medical bills.

It wasn't just finances. I had no emotional capacity, either.

Bitterness and the shame of failure had left my feelings bankrupt. Each crisis felt like being kicked after a beatdown. It reminded me of my loss and deepened my anxiety and depression. It was a downward spiral from which I saw no recovery.

There were times that I found it difficult to breathe. The metaphorical snakebite—which had poisoned me with bitterness—now enveloped me. With each successive setback, it tightened its grip around my chest.

Another bill was due. I felt the snake around another limb.

At the mall, I'd accidentally encounter someone I blamed for my situation. The snake squeezed tighter.

Car troubles or health issues arose. It became hard to breathe.

The ratcheting tension was nearing a breaking point. But I didn't know what was going to break.

It turns out it was our washing machine.

Night of the washing machine

Without any money in savings, we had no way to pay for this unexpected expense out-of-pocket. We had to finance it, which meant we'd be in even more debt.

I felt immobilized by shame and anger as the snake gripped tighter. Meanwhile, the poison flowed through my veins—waiting for the right moment to attack from the inside. So we put a new washing machine and dryer on financing and got them installed.

That night my wife, Tammy, and I fell asleep, knowing that at least one problem had been solved. The new debt we just incurred could wait until the morning.

Later that night, though, our son—the one who broke his arm—came into our room and woke us.

"It's raining downstairs," he said softly.

In a heartbeat, I knew what was wrong. I jumped up and rushed across the hall to our upstairs laundry room.

Splish! Splash! My feet landed in inches of water covering the floor. A hose behind the washing machine was spraying across the room. Frantically, I turned off the water. Tammy walked in, her eyes widening in realization. If the upstairs looked like this...

We ran down the steps to see water streaming through the dining room ceiling. I'd been working on my laptop earlier that evening. There it was, right in the middle of the dining room table, under a virtual Niagara—completely soaked and ruined.

I felt a pang of dread, knowing water damage on one floor can be costly, but this was multiple rooms upstairs and down. Did I say dread? I meant hopelessness.

Tammy and I stayed up most of the night sucking up water with a wet/dry vacuum and running fans to dry out the floors and ceiling the best we could. First thing in the morning, I called a disaster recovery company to bring in professional equipment and assess the damage.

Our one saving grace was the knowledge that the appliance installers were responsible for the leak. The hose was cross-threaded and popped loose in the night. At least, the financial burden would be shared.

The commercial insurer dashed our hopes by refusing to pay for the repairs. After months of haggling, they finally agreed to pay for half the carpet we had to replace. During that time, we had lived with our house torn apart since we couldn't pay for the repairs ourselves.

Begrudgingly, we agreed to their terms, even though we knew it meant additional debt. I didn't think the snake could wrap itself any tighter, but it ratcheted down even more.

I usually considered shopping to be enjoyable, but I didn't look forward to finding a new carpet. Resentment, this time for the commercial insurer, seethed within me. I felt like we were holding someone else's tab.

There I was, standing in the showroom of a carpet store—the toxic smell of carpet glue and nylon fibers saturating the air. A burly salesman helped us find a reasonably priced option. He was writing up an estimate for the carpet and installation when I noticed something strange.

As I stood there, my right foot was tingling. It felt like it was asleep. I shook it to see if the movement would circulate blood. A moment later, I realized my leg was numb to the calf muscle. After a few more minutes, the dull sensation reached my knee.

The poison of bitterness and blame—dormant for months—was now coursing through me, slowly paralyzing me. The mental and psychological toll I had carried with me was becoming physical. I felt trapped inside a sinking ship. It was one of the scariest moments of my life. And, in a second, it would also become so for my wife.

3

"How does one produce a climate in which people speak up, point out safety-related information, or correct their superiors when they are about to make a mistake?"

Edgar H. Schein, former professor at MIT

Blame
at Work

Reading the barometer

Every year, the global public relations firm Edelman publishes its Trust Barometer. This report shares worldwide survey data on the amount of trust people place in their government, the media, and businesses.

According to the 2022 survey, people were more fearful of losing their jobs than of losing their freedom, the threat of climate change, or experiencing racism. Many respondents (63%) say they were worried about being lied to by business leaders.

Along a similar line, according to a recent Gallup survey, only 60% of employees know their duties in the workplace. Nearly half don't know their responsibilities because their managers don't help them set goals. Without clear expectations, it's hard for employees to meet performance standards. Nobody seems to know what the point is. Add to that the blame they'll likely receive for not achieving these unspoken objectives and it's a volatile mix.

Putting all this together—concern for job security, lack of trust in management, and outright confusion about goals—creates a ripe environment for blame. We don't feel safe at work. We don't think our leaders will follow through on their promises. It's easy to see why workers are hesitant to admit mistakes.

These same factors contribute to work cultures that are rigid and restrictive. Employees don't feel free to suggest new ideas or take calculated risks that lead to innovation. Leaders struggle to generate engagement and collaboration from their teams.

Ultimately, everyone is looking out for themselves—protecting their own interests. This isolation creates an us-versus-them mindset that fuels blame, deteriorating a team's ability to add value.

Where trust is absent, blame is more than willing to fill the void. Blame hampers innovation. And it makes attracting and retaining talent more challenging. Who wants to work in a toxic culture?

Playing hot potato

I grew up in a beautiful rural area of Oklahoma with plenty of wide open plains. We lived roughly halfway between the two little towns, not close enough to be in either one.

One day, a neighbor's home down the road caught fire. The fire departments from each town arrived in time to fight the blaze. With all that manpower, you'd think they would've put it out twice as fast.

Nope. Since it wasn't clear which jurisdiction the home was in, the two fire chiefs argued vehemently over who should extinguish the blaze. They couldn't agree.

Meanwhile, the house burned down.

Who was to blame?

You could blame both fire chiefs. Or you could blame neither. Maybe a county official should've demarcated the township lines better, made their duties clear. But you'd have difficulty narrowing the responsibility down to one group, let alone to one individual.

The story didn't end there, though.

The raging fire had consumed the entire house. All that was left was a chimney. Perhaps out of comfort or practicality, our neighbors rebuilt their new home around the surviving brick chimney. From the road, it looked just like the old structure.

And, just like the old one, the new house also burned down.

An inspection uncovered the cause of both fires—the chimney.

In the first blaze, the fire departments didn't help the situation, but the ultimate cause of each blaze was a flaw in the chimney. Even if the crews had saved the original house, it would've burned down eventually.

This story sounds a little crazy. I wouldn't have believed it if I hadn't been there myself.

You know what's even crazier? This type of scenario happens in the workplace all the time.

Work is done. Decisions are made. Calculated risks are taken.

Plenty of people show up, but everyone plays it safe. They hide behind unclear roles and responsibilities. They avoid decisions and risk, fearing it will make them targets for blame.

Meanwhile, fires rage on as we avoid the problem. The house burns down. While we ignore the primary causes of our problems—focusing attention on a scapegoat—more flames ignite. The chimney is the flawed part of our workplace culture that's there all the time, so omnipresent that we've become blind to its negative impact.

Blame's psychological game of hot potato comes at a high cost. It's a price we can no longer afford to pay.

Driving with the brakes on

Several years ago, my wife Tammy and I drove our young family two hundred-plus miles from Tulsa, Oklahoma, to Dallas, Texas. It's a scenic drive through rural Oklahoma, passing near a few state parks. We were about halfway through the four-hour journey when, suddenly, our minivan seemed to seize up.

I decelerated instantly. Then I realized the vehicle could only go about five miles per hour, no matter how much I pressed the accelerator.

We had the van towed back to my cousin John's transmission shop in Tulsa, expecting to hear bad news. A new transmission would cost thousands of dollars. Needless to say, we didn't have that much savings at the time.

After giving it a once-over at the shop, John called. He surprised me when he explained that one of our brakes was not assembled correctly after a recent visit to the mechanic. The caliper had come loose and clamped down. We were driving with the brakes on. I was relieved that the fix was easy and much more affordable.

Unfortunately, at work, we tend to drive with the brakes on without noticing it. But since we're still inching forward at five miles an hour, it feels progressive, so we don't fix it.

Blame is a common culprit. It slows our progress, damaging the company as it lurches ahead. It creates systemic issues the longer we let it go unchecked.

Blame is an ineffective method for managing fear. It hampers creativity, collaboration, and leadership. You could say that blame is a workplace tool as common as computers, copiers, and staplers.

We blame others to ensure we don't get blamed ourselves.

Conversely, we condemn ourselves—throwing our case at the mercy of the court. We plead to get a reduced sentence, hoping the effects of blaming ourselves will be more palatable than waiting for someone else to point the finger.

Blame cultures facilitate toxic environments where individuals avoid responsibility and instead play an emotional game of hot potato. Blame is tossed from one person to the next until someone unlucky is left holding it when the buzzer sounds.

I mentioned before that using blame as a management tool repels talent. According to a survey by performance management software company Reflektive, 85% of workers say they'd consider quitting after an unfair performance review.

The data indicates that employees who feel unfairly blamed—or uncredited for success—are more likely to quit their job. In fact, the animosity goes deeper. More than three out of four workers wanted to create an 'I quit' video for social media, detailing—for the entire world—the toxic culture they endured.

That's not how we do things around here

So what's the alternative? Attention, feedback, and guidance from managers all help with employee engagement and retention. What effect does fear of blame have on creativity, productivity, and leadership development?

Innovation often requires deviating from established ideas and processes. Fear of blame inhibits our desire to try anything but the tried-and-true solutions. This is why many workplace cultures use the phrase, "That's not how we do things around here." It's a warning that you step outside the established norms at your own risk.

Part of the benefit of hiring employees from outside your organization is the wealth of new experiences they bring.

Fear of blame and a xenophobic work culture negates this benefit. Everyone wants to become a 'team player,' right? New team members are soon paralyzed—restraining themselves from contributing so they fit in.

And fear of blame galvanizes existing employees into the status quo. The entire team is unwilling to take risks or deviate from the norms because they don't want to be saddled with failure.

Remember, if "the way things are done around here" fails, it's nobody's fault. It's just the invisible inertia of tradition. No one is the scapegoat. Everyone feels safe. But this false sense of security comes at the expense of creativity and innovation.

Blame attacks

Another disturbing trend that workplace surveys reveal is the rise in personal attacks due to altercations at work. Not all conflict is avoidable. Of course leaders must address poor performance and unacceptable behavior in the workplace. But the objective should be to avoid making the issue personal through blame, shame, or guilt.

When conflict arises with a person, we tend to focus on personality and perceived agenda rather than on the common goals and challenges we share. This tendency makes it more likely we'll resort to ad hominem attacks or even physical violence because we see the individual as the problem instead of their behavior.

Blame takes our attention away from correcting behavior and focuses us on attempting to shame others into compliance. But what we really want is engagement. We want employees who dig into the work with vigor. People who are willing to put in extra effort when needed. They will take calculated risks and stick their neck out for a project to be successful.

Blame won't give us those results.

Taming a wild tiger

The workplace is a relatively modern development. Historically, human society has been primarily agrarian, working the land. Until recently, this work occurred on family farms. The traditional values of these families and their communities drove the broader culture.

The majority of what we consider 'work culture' developed within the 20th Century. The term was rare until the 1960s. It didn't become common until the surge in business books during the 1980s.

The pervasiveness of interest in—and references to—work culture has grown exponentially since then. But in the past few years, much of the intellectual foundation laid since the mid-20th Century has been reconsidered.

Initially, business culture was driven from the top down. However, as technology has flattened organizational structures and made communication instantaneous, culture is now decentralized. It is impacted far more by employees' perceptions than by any executive mandates or edict.

As leaders, work culture is out of our hands. It's a wild tiger. You have little hope of controlling it. A more appropriate goal might be to influence it instead.

With the disruption of command-and-control environments at work—and, since the COVID pandemic, with many employees opting to work at home, at least partially—corporate culture has become an even more popular subject for business leaders.

Meanwhile, everyone seems to have their own definition for this enigmatic term. I attended a presentation recently where the speaker asked the audience to define 'culture.' Most folks in the audience didn't even raise a hand. The ones that did offered answers which varied considerably. Is culture in the eye of the beholder?

How can we as leaders address cultures that are unproductive, un-engaging, or even openly hostile when we don't even have a common understanding of what a work culture actually is?

How habits power culture

While I was working in partnership with the commercial interiors giant Steelcase, their Workspace Futures research team described the difference between habit and culture:

Individual behavior over time equals a habit.
Group behavior over time equals culture.

This simple equation transformed the way I defined business culture. It's simply what we do over time as a group. Once behavior becomes accepted, it's not long before it's expected. The marketing guru Seth Godin coined an aphorism—"People like us do things like this." That's culture in a nutshell.

Thus, a blame culture is one where scapegoating is accepted and expected. No matter a new hire's intention, eventually they habituate into the organization's dominant culture—for better or worse.

An article in Harvard Business Review titled "The Blame Game" showed, through extensive research, the adverse effects of blame on those addicted to it. The writer concluded:

> "People who blame others for their mistakes lose status, learn less, and perform worse relative to those who own up to their mistakes."

In addition, the research showed the same consequences for organizations as a whole:

> "Groups and organizations with a rampant culture of blame have a serious disadvantage when it comes to creativity, learning, innovation, and productive risk-taking."

In his blockbuster book *The Power of Habit*, author Charles Duhigg identifies what he calls the Habit Loop. He found habits are a sequence of cues, routines, and rewards. A cue prompts us to follow a routine reinforced by a reward.

Marilyn Paul, Ph.D., an author and business consultant, found something similar with organizations. She calls it Cycles of Blame:

> "Blame causes fear, which increases cover-ups and reduces the flow of information. The lack of information hinders problem solving, creating more errors."

Like the Habit Loop, Cycles of Blame perpetuate themselves. Fear creates more mistakes—spawning more blame and instigating more fear.

Moreover, blame is not simply a cycle in two dimensions. It has a third dimension—depth. Blame creates a vicious downward spiral that consumes individuals and group cultures.

Blame destroys trust among peers, so groups don't have healthy relationships that help to mitigate fear. Without the undergirding of interpersonal trust, the downward spiral increases. Those wanting a healthier work culture inevitably have one choice—to leave.

When desire births blame

I mentioned René Girard discovered that the scapegoat mechanism was present in every society. But another of his frameworks inspired entrepreneur Peter Thiel to become an early investor in Facebook. Thiel recognized that the burgeoning social media platform was an online manifestation of Girard's mimetic theory.

With mimetics, Girard proposed that individuals in the same group develop desires for the same things. When that desire is for something rare, it creates rivalries and, inevitably, violence. This explains the centuries of wars and battles over land, power, and money. While these conflicts raged in the broader society, it's not hard to see another arena where this plays out—the workplace.

Renowned Belgian-American psychotherapist Esther Perel was asked to name what she thought was the most significant indicator of a toxic work environment. Her answer?

Contempt.

Leaders often use a mix of greed and envy to motivate employees. Unfortunately, these are perfect ingredients to foster contempt instead.

You might recall the monologue given by Alec Baldwin at the start of the film *Glengarry Glen Ross*. His character—a confident salesman named Blake—is supposed to inspire an office of lackluster-performing real estate agents with a competition. Near the end of his pitch, he employs the proverbial carrot and stick:

> *"As you all know, first prize is a Cadillac El Dorado. Anyone wanna see second prize?" Blake holds up a small box. "Second prize is a set of steak knives. Third prize is you're fired."*

Greed, shame, and fear of unemployment—what a rousing speech to the troops.

What contributes more contempt to our lives than envy and jealousy? Yet companies continue to encourage employees to pursue the same limited rewards. This tight competition creates the mimetic desire and conflict Girard referenced.

It's pretty common for multiple individuals to want the same job role. Buildings only have so many vertices to create those coveted corner offices. Power and status are reserved for select positions. As in *Glengarry Glen Ross*, commissions and other incentives are afforded only to top performers.

This survival of the fittest mentality creates artificial scarcity to manufacture urgency and motivation. Unfortunately, it comes at the expense of the workplace culture. Teammates become rivals, and— without a healthy sense of shared purpose—they develop contempt for one another.

Concerning relationships, psychologist John Gottman listed contempt as one of the Four Horsemen of the Apocalypse. The other three included criticism, defensiveness, and stonewalling.

It's been said that familiarity breeds contempt. Maybe this is because, as we get to know a person better, we abandon our curiosity about them. We assume we already know their habits, reasons, and unspoken motives.

But, c'mon. The truth is, when we assume to know why someone did something we disagree with, we're guessing. We have no way of knowing their motive unless they honestly tell us. This is why we assume the worst of people we know best, even those we have worked with closely. Familiarity, unfortunately, breeds contempt.

The Facebook paradox

It makes sense that we could harbor contempt for our colleagues. We can see how the same psychological trap that makes Facebook a tinderbox of polarized accusations and hatred is at play in our offices.

As much as we talk about hating Facebook and the bickering it creates, we have a hard time avoiding it. We're even worse at avoiding toxic workplaces.

Transforming our habits and our culture is uncomfortable. It means we may face embarrassment. We may have to do what is right and true. It could mean difficult conversations to confront others abusing blame. It may mean taking action when doing nothing seems easier. Finally, kicking the blame habit means we might give up our perceived status and sense of control.

In all these circumstances, we have to choose discomfort over the status quo. Author Brené Brown says something related:

> "Choose discomfort over resentment. Compassionate people ask for what they need. They say no when they need to, and when they say yes, they mean it."

Sometimes, we are choosing whether or not to resent others. Other times, we may be deciding whether or not to resent ourselves.

The bottom line is that we need to be intentional.

Unless we intentionally identify and root out the blame habit, we will tolerate and contribute to the cultivation of a blame culture.

Are you willing to choose discomfort over resentment?

Blame, diversity, and inclusion

It is not my goal to address Diversity, Equity, and Inclusion (DEI) programs in general. Still, with the prevalence of DEI efforts across the business world, it is helpful to see the role of blame in this field.

First, leaders who wish to have a diverse and inclusive workforce must acknowledge how minority groups have historically been affected by blame. Many people have been used as scapegoats in the past. They've been blamed for everything from poverty and job losses to moral corruption and wars.

Knowing this has been the pattern for centuries, why would anyone from a historically-marginalized group expect the present to be any different?

Second, as DEI programs are planned and facilitated, leaders should be careful that blame is not transferred to a different group of people. In my opinion, many leading DEI programs make assertions about white people which can swing the pendulum of blame to the opposite extreme. Moreover, this counter-balancing is intentional.

Take, for example, the common practice of starting DEI training by talking about the concept of white privilege. Though intended to motivate people to change their behavior, this practice can create a sense of shame or misperception in white participants—shutting them down emotionally. No actual progress is possible.

Blaming a group of people—for the actions of a few individuals—does not lead to change, even when the shoe is on the other foot.

If the goal of a program is to foster inclusivity, then it should not weaponize resentment and aim it at another group. It shouldn't shame participants based on their personhood or unchangeable characteristics. This approach leads to defensiveness from those feeling attacked. Ultimately, it doesn't create inclusion. It creates more division.

We described blame as resentment we feel toward those we hold at fault. So, when we set up programs that do just that, we shouldn't be surprised when they fail to create unity or a healthy culture.

Does this mean that we shouldn't strive for diversity and inclusion? Are DEI programs fundamentally flawed? Of course not.

Racism, sexism, and discrimination based on sexual orientation or gender identity are wrong. Full stop. Many in these groups have been unfairly maligned for too long a time. However, using blame as a tool to justify these historical inequities is not going to heal the wounds. It only will continue to divide us and hurt people based on our differences.

The solution to injustice shouldn't be doing the same thing, simply in reverse.

Thankfully, there are advocates with approaches that avoid weaponizing resentment and blame. They understand that, to move forward, people must accept responsibility for their part in the problem. Even more importantly, we must take an active part in finding a solution together.

For DEI programs to be successful, they can't make one group the enemy. Instead, they need to focus on how we can work together to create a more just and equitable workplace. One that doesn't rely on blame.

PART 2

Blaming Others

4

"*The man who can smile when things go wrong
has thought of someone else he can blame it on.*"

Robert Bloch, author of the novel *Psycho*

The Seduction
of Blame

The Blame Contagion

No one likes to be blamed, but we often have little issue with blaming others. It's a double standard.

As they say, we want justice for others but mercy for ourselves.

Part of the reason is that our intentions are internal. We know our own motives, but we assume the motives of others. And, usually, we assume the worst.

That's the most straightforward conclusion, but it isn't always the most accurate or the most generous. People make mistakes. If we inadvertently hurt someone, we know what we intended to do. So we give ourselves grace. Yet, we seek justice when another person errs because we assume their underlying intentions must be malicious.

This perspective infects our workplace. USC and Stanford professors conducted experiments, studying how blame spreads among team members. They coined it the Blame Contagion.

Their research concluded that people who observed someone blaming another person in their organization often went on to do the same thing. The participants in the study didn't have to be the victim of blame, just an observer. That was enough to influence their future actions. In fact, the research even showed that participants who read stories involving blame increased the likelihood of using blame in their interactions.

The BP Oil Spill is an excellent example of the Blame Contagion. When Tony Hayworth, the CEO of BP, skirted responsibility for his company's actions, it set a standard of behavior. BP was the lead entity in the incident. Soon other smaller organizations involved with the disaster followed suit. Passing the buck was the norm.

In cases of highly publicized scandals like this, the spread of the blame is more pronounced. Leaders often use public relations and other media professionals to point fingers elsewhere. Are you willing to choose discomfort over resentment?

Adding shame to blame

But the Blame Contagion is more subtle in less public incidents. Recently, in Ghana, research showed how a culture of blame led to poor healthcare results in some of the hospitals. Aaron Asibi Abuosi, an Associate Professor of Health Policy and Management at the University of Ghana Business School, was investigating the issue.

In one example, a nurse shared a secret with the professor. He recalls, "she mistakenly gave xylocaine (an anesthetic) instead of normal saline, both clear liquids, to a child. The child died. The nurse confided in her colleagues, and they collectively decided not to report the fatal mistake for fear of any negative consequences."

But this type of coverup isn't just an issue in Ghana. Professor Abuosi also tells the story of Kimberly Hiatt at Seattle Children's Hospital in Washington state. As a pediatric nurse treating a child with a heart problem, she accidentally gave her patient ten times the required dose of calcium chloride. The child died because of this, and Hiatt was terminated. Unable to cope with her mistake, the shamed nurse committed suicide six months later.

Speaking at an intercollegiate lecture, Abuosi mentioned Hiatt's excellent record and reputation as an experienced nurse for twenty-four years in Seattle. Despite the tragic loss of a child's life, he wondered whether firing the nurse was the correct response:

> *"Do you think other nurses or doctors who commit similar errors will own up after her dismissal if they make any mistake? And if they don't own up, how can hospitals know the errors and take steps to avoid their recurrence?"*

Entire institutions are robbed of organizational learning when blame culture persists. Skilled and sorely needed talent is lost, not just by the hospital but the industry at large, when they see the risks they might bear for any possible imperfection.

This example highlights how challenging it is to avoid the contagion of blame spreading at work. Even when a few people are infected with the blame virus, it can spread rapidly.

Bullies and false victims

Blaming others, obviously, involves power. What's less obvious is how that maneuver can come from two different positions:

1. A position of abusive power
2. A position of perceived oppression

The blamer is typically either a bully or a false victim.

Bullies blame from a position of abusive power. This strategy is an attempt to either retain power or gain more of it.

To retain power, the bully blames someone with little power. This keeps the scapegoat in a weakened position so they cannot assume control, stealing it from the bully. For example, a manager may blame one of their direct reports to keep them from asking for a promotion or raise. Or the bully might want the person to feel so incompetent they cannot pursue a different job. A bully leader uses blame to keep subordinates in their place.

To gain power, the bully will blame someone with a semblance of power—possibly comparable to themselves. This tactic is to avoid sharing control with the scapegoat or to avoid them gaining more power than the bully. It reasserts the bully's desire to be the alpha dog. An example is a VP of Marketing blaming a failure on another department, avoiding any blemishes on their leadership, and casting aspersions on someone else's.

Bullies use blame as a weapon.

Conversely, false victims blame from a position of perceived oppression. They are deniers of their agency. Yes, bad things have happened to them, but never because of their own doing. A false victim demands affirmation of their worldview from others.

Claiming victimhood while blaming others allows this person to maintain a sense of moral superiority. Others have done them wrong. Justice is now needed.

The exact opposite of bullies, false victims always blame those they perceive to have more power. This allows them to gain pseudo-power from the scapegoat while avoiding any responsibility.

Assigning blame to another makes a statement of one's status. It adds to the stigma of being blamed and the appeal of scapegoating others. Moreover, we often assign blame because of status.

A hint of narcissism

In ancient days, the human scapegoat was nearly always a peasant, a beggar, a prostitute, or a person with a disease. The assumption was this person was already cursed in some way. They were destined, by the gods, to suffer. They must have done something wrong or be a bad person to deserve such a fate. Therefore, their fellow citizens felt no remorse for casting them from society.

However, the wealthy and powerful occasionally receive blame, but only when they are deemed morally inferior. This assessment of one's soul is another form of status. At times, more important than wealth or power. Yet, even if the scapegoat is immoral, basing judgment on their character ignores whether or not the individual is responsible for the offense in question.

Odd as it may sound, when we blame a high-status person, we're more likely to scapegoat someone innocent. Diminishing their status serves as confirmation bias, reinforcing our decision. We take glee in bringing down the powerful, whether they deserve or not.

While speaking at the South by Southwest conference a few years ago, psychotherapist Esther Perel discussed the personalities of the bully and the victim. Her observation is that bullies never perceive anything as being their fault. Meanwhile, victims seem to blame themselves for everything:

> "What's interesting about this is that both of these reactions share a similar grandiosity. In one situation, you are also fantastic, and in the other, you are also terrible. But both share the same hint of narcissism."

That is the rub. As different as bullies and false victims appear on the surface, they are very similar deep down. They are both narcissists who will never take personal responsibility but rather will deflect blame and ensure it lands on the person whose demise most benefits themselves.

Self-protecting vs. self-destructing

Blame is not productive. Blame disguises and conceals. Blame alienates and separates. Blame is the killer of community, cooperation, and collaboration.

Peter Rouse, Counselor to the President

What is the best way to manage failure? In the 1930s, psychologist Saul Rosenzweig conducted a study on how people experience anger and frustration. He identified three common responses:

1. Impunitive—minimizing or denying failure
2. Extrapunitive—blaming others unfairly for failure
3. Intropunitive—judging oneself for nonexistent failure

Rosenzweig's choice of clinical terms doesn't roll off the tongue in everyday conversation. So, instead, let's refer to his concepts about blame as minimizing, externalizing, and internalizing.

The motivation behind minimizing blame may seem obvious. Often, we seek freedom from punishment. We don't want to suffer the consequence of our failure. If we accept this responsibility, we're also admitting we need to change. But avoiding responsibility has a seductive hook. It's easier to convince others that there's no problem, and fool ourselves as well. Thus, we maintain our inner status quo.

Externalizing blame is attributing fault to outside forces—such as people, situations, or circumstances. We criticize, resent, and seek to punish others. We externalize to protect ourselves. It can be an effort to save face or an excuse to escape blame. We don't have to accept responsibility or change our behavior when externalizing.

When we internalize, we blame ourselves for whatever went wrong and any related adverse outcomes. In this case, we avoid shifting blame or responsibility to someone else, even if that would be more reasonable. Internalizing can lead to taking responsibility for outcomes we had no control over.

Moreover, internalizing blame is self-destructive. It breeds self-doubt, perfectionism, and low self-esteem. This type of behavior is often associated with depression and anxiety.

Self-destructing behavior strives for unattainable perfection. We judge ourselves harshly when we don't meet those unrealistic standards. It leads to guilt and shame. Additionally, it can have long-term negative effects on our health.

Assuming the worst in others

In May 2016, on a bright sunny afternoon at the Cincinnati Zoo, a three-year-old boy wandered away from his family and climbed over a short barrier to the gorilla habitat. The curious youngster traversed along a few feet of dense shrubbery, then—unexpectedly—tumbled down a rock ledge fifteen feet into a shallow moat.

Immediately zoo personnel sprung into action. They signaled for the three gorillas in the habitat to come back inside. The two female apes complied. Unfortunately, a 440-pound silverback male named Harambe wanted to investigate the commotion in the moat.

At first, the immense creature, an endangered western lowland gorilla, seemed curious and even protective of the young boy. But as zoo visitors screamed with fright from the top of the enclosure, Harambe exhibited defensive behavior. Possibly seeking to protect the child, the gorilla aggressively dragged the boy by the foot several yards within the moat.

For ten agonizing minutes, officials assessed the deteriorating situation as the gorilla became increasingly agitated. Ultimately, they decided there was only one option to protect the young child's life—killing the ape.

With a single rifle shot, Harambe dropped dead to the ground; the traumatized boy still near his feet.

The tragic and violent loss of a critically endangered species sparked outrage among the public. The fallout lasted for weeks. Some people blamed the zoo for their decision to kill Harambe. Others blamed the child's mother, as they perceived she was not providing adequate supervision over her three-year-old.

Though many in the media were unkind—using the controversy to ignite outrage in their audience—cable news commentator Mel Robbins made a case for empathy instead of blame:

> "What if instead of lawyering up and assigning blame like we always do, we take a step back in this instance and try a little empathy? The parents didn't throw the kid into the enclosure, the crowd didn't mean to agitate Harambe, and the zoo didn't want to have to kill him."

Though deeply saddened by the tragedy, primate research scientist Jane Goodall supported the zoo's decision, as did wildlife expert Jack Hannah. He said shooting a tranquilizer instead of a live round wouldn't have been effective since the medication can take five to ten minutes to sedate a giant ape. The boy's life was of higher importance, and every second counted in the volatile situation.

And if anyone is a lover of—and advocate for—our ape cousins, it is Goodall. Surely her endorsement would change people's minds. But critics in the echo chamber of the internet were not convinced.

An online petition titled "Justice for Harambe" garnered over half a million signatures. The supporters felt the mother should be held responsible. They pressured officials to investigate whether she neglected to watch over her son appropriately. The petition read:

> This beautiful gorilla lost his life because the boy's parents did not keep a closer watch on the child. We the undersigned believe that the child would not have been able to enter the enclosure under proper parental supervision.

After investigating the incident, the local county prosecutor Joseph Deter tried to defuse criticism of the mother. Deter reminded the public that the mom had three other children with her at the time, commenting that, "If anyone doesn't believe a three-year-old can scamper off very quickly, they've never had kids."

In the aftermath

Yet this pragmatism is not a satisfying conclusion to a tragedy. A gorilla lost its life. His crime? Just being a wild animal held captive in Cincinnati. Someone must pay. Someone has to take the blame.

We seem to have a transactional sense of justice. To quote the Book of Exodus: "An eye for an eye. A tooth for a tooth."

But what if nobody did anything malicious?

Should a mother be held responsible for an accident caused by her child's curiosity? Should zoos no longer hold apes captive, even though they are a source of education and connection with our primate relatives?

In complex scenarios like these, we know there isn't a single, isolated source of blame. But, deep down, we still crave a scapegoat.

Harambe himself became an icon of the search for justice. Some attempted to connect the tragedy of his death with the Black Lives Matter movement. Others used Harambe's martyrdom as a symbol of the downtrodden and oppressed.

In October 2021, a seven-foot bronze statue was erected in New York City, placing the seated simian directly opposite Wall Street's famous Charging Bull. The patrons of the new sculpture questioned the Financial District's motives, which they said: "enriches wealthy elites and leaves the average person behind."

Pointing the finger of blame at someone else gives us a false sense of self-worth. We effectively say, "I would never do something like that." It also gives us something to do with the negative feelings associated with the incident.

In the case of Harambe, we may feel sadness that the gorilla was killed. We may also feel a sense of injustice in his death. It seemed pointless and unnecessary.

If only the boy didn't crawl into the habitat.

If only the zoo had better security.

If only the mother were in control of the situation.

The more we hear about it on cable news networks and read the social media posts echoing the sadness and anger, the more these emotions build within us. We need an outlet for all of this venom swelling inside. Pointing our finger at a scapegoat feels like opening a safety valve on a pipe ready to burst. But, actually, we are releasing poison into our bodies instead.

Heaping shame and criticism upon someone doesn't necessarily solve any problems. It doesn't bring any healing. It doesn't promote growth. Still, there's an innate desire to attack those we hold at fault.

Until we acknowledge that and call blame out by name, we will continue to fall victim to the Blame Loop.

Blaming the bogeyman

I think it's too easy often to find a villain out of the headlines and to then repeat that villainy again and again and again. You know, traditionally, America has always looked to scapegoat someone as the boogie man.

Edward Zwick
Film Director, *Legends of The Fall*

Politicians are masters of taking something with little to no power and magnifying it to seem like an existential threat to our safety and livelihood. In the U.S., Republicans present the liberal agenda as a danger to family values. Democrats use identity politics to paint their opponents as a menace to civil rights. Both parties portray the other is a threat to democracy.

While these claims may be rooted in truth, each side takes the rhetoric to hyperbolic levels to motivate their political base to take action. Creating this oppositional energy is pretty simple, yet it is highly effective.

That's why con artists use the same tactics. It creates a dividing line between them and us. Grifters want you to identify as one of 'us' and then detail how the enemy is out to harm 'our' group. This is why the cable network talk shows spew such hyperbolic accusations of catastrophic consequences if the opposition gets its way. "They want to destroy America! Our way of life!"

In the extreme, the demonizing of one political party by the other leads to many people accepting wildly outlandish ideas.

For example, on a Sunday afternoon in December 2016, a family-friendly restaurant in Washington, D.C., was packed with customers. That's when Edgar Maddison Welch walked through the doors of a local restaurant called Comet Pizza.

The 28-year-old North Carolina man was holding an AR-15 assault rifle. He told customers to evacuate and pointed his weapon toward a male employee who ran outside, fearing for his life.

After spending more than twenty minutes in the restaurant,

Welch decided to surrender. He walked out with his hands in the air where awaiting officers quickly arrested him. Officials later claimed it was practically a miracle no one was even injured.

Welch claimed he wanted to 'self-investigate' reports the tiny pizza shop was home to a child-trafficking, pedophile ring. He needed to verify online rumors claiming Hillary Clinton and other Democrats had secret tunnels under the restaurant where they hid children and performed sadistic rituals.

The news media dubbed the incident Pizzagate. It was the unfortunate result of conspiracy theories that spread in the wake of the 2016 U.S. Presidential Election. Perhaps the rumors were an attempt to encourage Republican voters to show up at the polls and stop Hillary Clinton from winning the race. But the consequence of this baseless story nearly ended in tragedy.

There's no monopoly on conspiracies

Conspiracy theories are not exclusive to one party. They exist across the political spectrum, vilifying Republicans as well as Democrats.

One example is the theory that President George W. Bush and his administration were involved in the 9/11 attacks on the World Trade Center and Pentagon. The supposed motive? To justify later invading the Middle East.

Meanwhile, in the past few years, anti-vaccination conspiracies (related and unrelated to COVID-19) are spread by various groups: ultra-conservatives, health and wellness fanatics, InfoWars radio host Alex Jones, and anti-government groups. Their villains can range from Big Pharma to individuals such as Dr. Anthony Fauci and Microsoft founder Bill Gates.

The use of false bogeymen becomes an exercise in crying wolf.

The effect is two-fold.

Short-term, the disinformation creates extreme and dangerous reactions such Pizzagate and riots—like those in Kenosha, WI, and the U.S. Capitol.

Long-term, we become desensitized by people repeatedly raising the conspiracy flag, and we eventually fail to recognize when actual threats emerge. Foreign enemies and domestic terrorists fly under the radar of the public.

Similarly, we are prone to creating internal fights over peaceful national anthem protests or people wishing their customers a simple "Merry Christmas."

There's a reason why we call it a culture war. While the core issues being debated are important, our inability to hold civil discussions with respect for each other has gotten out of hand. We see the other side of the aisle as our enemy instead of recognizing the freedoms, structures, and processes that created the arena in which we compete. If we do not reign in the unjustified demonization of our opponents, we risk tearing down the foundations of our democracy.

Ironically, inciting fear of bogeymen who will bring about a crisis becomes a self-fulfilling prophecy by creating the problem itself.

Ultimately, creating these hyperbolic villains is simply a way of justifying blame. We are vilifying someone and portraying them as blameworthy to generate support for ourselves. In reality, this pseudo-solution creates even more significant problems by distracting us from real answers to our issues while fabricating fear that too often ends in violence.

Hollywood typically avoids creating simplistic villains because audiences don't find them believable. Yet, it seems we too easily believe those who oppose our views could themselves be pure evil incarnate.

5

"*Freedom is the only worthy goal in life. It is won by disregarding things that lie beyond our control.*"

Epictetus, 2nd Century Greek Philosopher

Fighting for Control

5

The myth of redemptive violence

The term 'culture war' can be a rallying cry for particular causes. It can work us up emotionally. The problem with this call to battle is that it reinforces the myth of redemptive violence.

As first described by theologian and author Walter Wink, the myth purports that violence is a necessary and effective means of resolving conflict. This age-old belief is used to justify aggression, warfare, and other forms of social control. Wink writes:

> "[The myth] enshrines the belief that violence saves,
> that war brings peace, that might makes right. It is one of
> the oldest continuously repeated stories in the world."

Why is this fallacy so successful? Wink argues that to us it seems inevitable—laced into our DNA. It's simply cause and effect. If one group commits violence on another, the action will be reciprocated. The only way to stop violence is to become hostile yourself.

The theologian shared a creation story from ancient Babylon in which the universe was formed from a single vicious act of revenge. The Babylonians claimed that humanity was saved by violence and, more disturbingly, born into it as an inheritance.

Mayhem is all around us. It is inevitable. It is inescapable.

Violence is who we are. It is our origin and our destiny.

In the workplace context, the myth of redemptive violence can be seen as a justification for blaming others for our own failings. The hostility created by blame may not always manifest externally, but it inflicts internal pain upon others. Using guilt to deal with failures is a destructive and flawed approach. It creates resentment and, at times, can even escalate into physical violence.

Wink shared another story about a complaining pastor. In the pastor's church, his nemesis—a much older man—needed to be in on every decision. In truth, the pastor had the same tendency. When asked why, the pastor explained that if things went wrong, he'd be blamed. He feared everything would fall apart. The pastor was scared that he'd end up an unloved failure. Then he was asked to identify why his nemesis, the older fellow, desired so much control. It was then the pastor reflected with clarity:

> "He's a retired farmer who milked five hundred cows a day. That's a big operation. He's sixty-six and just turned the farm over to his son. I think he feels his life is slipping away from him. And here I come trying to force him to release control of the whole church, too."

How did the pastor reach this insight? Empathy. The ability to understand another person's feelings is required to diffuse blame.

In this case, it illuminated how two men on opposite sides of a struggle were striving for the same thing—control. But a very specific type of control. Neither man actually wanted to control the other. What each wanted was control of their own life.

We naturally want to avoid losing a sense of agency. Some even say suffering is anytime we realize we have no control. And we do not enjoy suffering. Yet we will try to hold onto some sense of authority and autonomy by taking it from others.

If we're sincere, we realize none of us have a complete grip on our lives or the circumstances around us. Like the pastor, we can consider how our actions threaten someone else's sense of control and autonomy. By recognizing this much, we can respond to others with empathy instead of hostility.

We can choose to not let redemptive violence be our birthright.

Inhibiting others

We use blame to retain control over our own lives and likewise to control others. Blamers maintain the status quo by keeping people in their place, guarding the hierarchy of power.

This is why some family members sometimes react negatively to a relative trying to lose weight or gain financial independence. It upsets the existing balance. The status quo is a cultural gravity of sorts. It requires an enormous effort, an escape velocity, to accelerate beyond the stifling expectations within some families.

Why do we do this each other?

Often it starts with inhibiting ourselves first.

I was finishing grocery shopping recently, and the register lines were long. I chose the shortest one. After a while, I noticed my line was the slowest of all. Tension rose within me. I felt like Charlie Brown, pondering why this kind of thing always happens to me. Growing alongside that mounting unease was a desire for change.

But I didn't want my line to move faster.

Selfishly, I wanted all the other lines to go slower.

I asked myself why I cared how fast the other lines were going?

Firstly, they reminded me that I had made the wrong choice. Watching all the other people stepping closer toward their registers made me feel foolish, even though I couldn't predict how fast each customer would complete their purchases.

Secondly, I blamed those people for my misfortune. I wouldn't envy them if they weren't moving so fast. Man, I wished each of their lines came to standstill. Their good fortune created my desire for *schadenfreude* (the German word for getting pleasure from the misfortune of others). I sensed their troubles would bring me joy.

Honestly, it's an embarrassing story to tell. Still, our tendency to inhibit others isn't restricted to those with good fortune.

Suppression isn't a solution

Crystal Mason helped her husband run a tax preparation business near Dallas, TX. She was charged with and convicted of inflating her clients' tax refunds. When caught, Mason pleaded guilty. For her part, she was sentenced to five years in federal prison.

After four years, she was granted supervised release for the last twelve months of her sentence. She had owned her mistakes and accepted her consequences. Now, she was putting the pieces back together and returning to normalcy. This included her duty to vote in the upcoming election.

She showed up to her polling place to cast her vote and provided her ID, but a volunteer could not find her name on the rolls. As Mason began to leave, the volunteer offered her a provisional ballot, noting that it wouldn't count if she wasn't supposed to vote there.

Unbeknownst to Mason, she was ineligible to vote, since her sentence for felony tax fraud hadn't been completed. In contrast to those who receive parole or probation, individuals are not given official instructions about voting eligibility when placed on supervised release.

Mason assumed she could vote. This assumption would come back to haunt her.

Around that time, the State of Texas—in response to perceived voter fraud issues—had taken a hardline in prosecuting voting irregularities. The polling volunteer reported Mason's provisional ballot, noting he thought she was still serving her felony sentence.

Mason was arrested and given a plea deal that would have put her back in prison for violating the terms of her release. She rejected the deal because her violation was out of ignorance not malice.

However, Mason was convicted. The prosecution requested a stern punishment to send a message. The court sentenced her to five years in prison again. She served nine months for violation of her prison release and is appealing her conviction as of this writing.

Was Crystal Mason a scapegoat for Texas' new strict policies?

Voting rights proponents think so. They claim her plight is an example of sacrificing individuals without the power to appease a public outcry for justice. On the other hand, public officials pointed to the case an example of widespread election fraud.

But the facts didn't bear out this claim. Most of the convictions were unrelated incidents. Many cases were simple mistakes made by voters with no criminal intent. By definition, these are instances of 'voter fraud,' but not a highly coordinated conspiracy to disrupt the election as many politicians wanted to pretend.

But the facts didn't stop the partisan attempt to erect additional election laws. Some of the proposed changes threatened to convolute what is legal and illegal. The result, opponents claimed, would make it more likely that innocent mistakes could persist. They said the proposed laws might amount to voter suppression because it would frighten citizens who were formerly migrant, people with previous legal issues, and other less powerful groups on the margins.

These type of groups are prime targets for scapegoating.

First, they involve individuals with perceived lower status.

Second, the root cause of the problem (voter fraud) is being ignored while a dominant group seeks to assign blame to someone they consider to be blameworthy and conveniently expendable.

We often opt for a scapegoat instead of an objective analysis of the failure at hand. The typical result is that we further inhibit others without contributing to justice or real solutions.

Scapegoats on aisle 13

Let's journey back to the 1970s, a time of disco, *Star Wars*, and pet rocks. For ten years, Bernie Marcus was the CEO of Handy Dan, a chain of 44 home improvement stores on the West Coast.

Though Handy Dan was profitable, its parent company, Daylin, had underperforming assets like a drugstore chain. In 1975, Daylin filed for Chapter 11 bankruptcy. As a result, it was purchased by Sanford Sigoloff, an investor known for cleaning house to cut costs—including the senior executives. At the time, Marcus felt he was safe because Handy Dan made so much money.

He was wrong.

Sigoloff was combative; his work style was abrasive. Reportedly, he had a personality conflict with Bernie and another Handy Dan executive, Arthur Blank. By '78, things had reached a boiling point. Sigoloff fired them. The official reason given was for "unauthorized and unacceptable business practices."

Marcus said they were blamed for allowing the improper use of funds to fight a union but the charges were trumped up as an excuse.

Fortunately for Marcus and Blank, a Daylin board member approached them and offered to support a new business model for home improvement stores. One Bernie had been dreaming of.

Cut to the chase: Marcus and Blank created Home Depot, one of the world's largest home improvement brands.

This story gives us two lessons regarding blame.

First, we cannot let blame dictate our success. When others unfairly blame and use us as scapegoats, it doesn't define who we are or our future. Marcus and Blank didn't let their dismissal discourage them from reentering the home improvement store industry.

When we are blamed, it can feed into our imposter syndrome, making us feel inadequate. In reality, we're still the same person we were before being scapegoated. The blame is just one data point, which should be considered among many other forms of feedback we have received. Our assessment of ourselves and our abilities must be more than isolated instances of blame or praise.

Second, if we unfairly blame others, we may be inhibiting our success as much as—or even more than—the success of others. Marcus and Blank were already testing their ideas for a new business model for home improvement stores.

If they had not been blamed and fired, Home Depot could have become a flagship chain under the Daylin portfolio. As of 2022, the corporation consisted of over 2,300 stores worth over $300 billion. Meanwhile, Handy Dan went out of business in 1989.

Thunderstruck

When we respond to mistakes by seeking out who to blame, we tend to oversimplify the issue to narrow the blame to a select few. We may ignore systemic problems and external factors that contributed to the failure. In the end, blame is a blunt tool that rarely helps us to understand the root cause of the issue.

Thus, we are unlikely to find a solution. We may make the same mistakes again; experience the same failures later.

It would be great to focus on responsibility and accountability instead of blame. But in most workplaces, this is an uphill battle until we change the culture. Too many organizations allow tensions to rise until there is a discharge of blame.

After a failure, the environment is supercharged, like the climate during a thunderstorm. Dark clouds of negative energy swirl above, looking for a place to strike. Eventually, the negative energy builds up enough to be discharged. The target is usually one that sticks out from everything else. Once lightning strikes, it releases some of the pressure. At least until that negative energy builds back up.

Here is the critical difference between blame and responsibility. Blame seeks to relieve pressure, while responsibility aims to actually rectify the problem.

After a mistake, we need to consider whether our next steps are an attempt to resolve the issue. Our judgment becomes clouded by all kinds of hardwired internal responses. We could feel attacked, threatened, and unsafe. We may also feel angry or vengeful. Others may make us feel like they expect us to respond swiftly and firmly.

Our personal history or the company's culture may establish a track record for assigning blame and taking action. These are the moments we can't conflate the pressure with the problem.

Hot coffee on a pink sweater

Researcher and author Brené Brown shared a personal example of using blame to discharge our discomfort and pain.

She recounted a story when she was at home alone when she dropped a cup of hot coffee. It broke and splashed all over her white pants and pink sweater. Her first thought was, "Damn you, Steve." Brené's husband, Steve, had gotten home late the night before. This, in turn, had kept Brené up later than normal. Therefore, she was tired that morning, leading to her dropping a cup of coffee.

While cleaning up the mess, Steve happened to call. His timing was quite unfortunate. He asked her what was going on. To which she responded with annoyance, "What's going on? I'll tell you exactly what's going on. I'm cleaning up the coffee that spilled all over...."

Brené was met with the sound of a dial tone. Steve hung up. He knew he'd walked into something he wanted no part of.

As Brené shares her story, it is comical. Not because it is bizarre but because it's so common.

When something terrible happens, we immediately look for someone to blame. Sometimes those we love the most are the ones who accidentally walk right into our crosshairs. And sometimes, as Brown admits, it's even ourselves.

"I'd rather it be my fault than no one's fault. Why? Because it gives us some semblance of control. Here's what we know from the research, blame is simply the discharging of discomfort and pain. It has an inverse relationship with accountability. Blaming is a way that we discharge anger."

Here were are again. Blame is a release of pressure. It's a way to get rid of the intense anger that builds inside of us. So, why doesn't blame work? Because as mentioned earlier, this is simply a game of hot potato. We aren't genuinely getting rid of the pressure. We're trying to hand it off to someone else.

Steve was aware of this. That's why he made a hasty exit from a potentially harmful phone call. He wasn't going to play the game. We could all benefit from learning a thing or two from Steve.

"Am I dying?"

Let's go back to the carpet store. When we last left our hapless hero, my foot had gone strangely asleep. Then a numb sensation crept up the entire limb. I told my wife, Tammy, my leg was asleep. I was going to try walking it off. I did for a couple of minutes, but the numbness kept climbing, reaching my waist.

"This is serious," I thought. I told Tammy I'd call the doctor's office to seek advice. By the time I got ahold of a nurse, the ribs on my right side were without feeling. I asked if I should make an appointment with the doctor. The nurse stated emphatically, "No! You need to get to the closest emergency room right now."

Tammy drove me to a nearby hospital. By then, the numbness had reached the top of my head. It was like a line was drawn right down the center of my body from head to toe. The right half of my body was without feeling, while the left side was normal. This was a bad sign. Thankfully, we were pulling into the hospital parking lot.

I spotted a parking spot near the E.R. entrance. I tried to tell Tammy. "Mpharksspohht." The words came out as gibberish.

Suddenly, fear grabbed me. I realized the one-sided numbness and speech impediment were indicators of something terrible—I was having a stroke. I wondered if this was how my life would end.

Am I dying? I thought.

It all became a blur

I had never experienced anything like this before. I had no control over my own body or mind. Something was going wrong, and I was helpless to do anything.

My life didn't flash before my eyes, but I considered Tammy's possibility of becoming a widow. I realized I might not get to grow old with her. I thought of my three young children—becoming teens and then adults without me as a part of their lives. Would I see them graduate, marry, or have their kids? It was a crushing reality, and it scared me more than anything.

Not only was I scared, but I was baffled. My mind intermittently lost its ability to process information. Because of this, much of what happened next is a blur to me.

I had difficulty walking into the emergency room.. Tammy brought me in, and the staff asked me questions—simple things that I had trouble answering. When I managed to speak, I gave the wrong information. I forgot my birthday, my address. Tammy had to answer because I could no longer function.

The staff put me into a triage room until I could be examined.

Then things got worse.

An excruciating headache hit me like a sledgehammer. Within minutes, I felt like someone had inserted a bicycle pump into my head and started pumping. My head felt like it expanded to the point of explosion with each pulse of unreal pain.

I was overcome with nausea while experiencing the relentless attack on my body. Standard painkillers didn't relieve me, so the doctors put me on a morphine drip. But, even with the morphine, I was writhing in pain.

I curled into the fetal position, holding my head as my legs continued churning. It was as if my body was continually moving, searching for a place where the pain would stop. I cried for more morphine, but the doctor told Tammy I was getting the maximum dosage they could safely give me. It was hell.

Eventually, I fell asleep.

Maybe it was the dull drip of the morphine or perhaps just the fatigue of fighting the pain. I was happy to slip the bonds of my body.

That night, the doctors diagnosed the attack as a ministroke.

They told Tammy they fully expected me to recover, but they weren't sure if I would regain all of my functions. There was no way of knowing. When I woke up the next morning, my wife had no idea if I would able to walk, talk, or even feed myself.

For both of us, this was one of those moments where life holds the possibility of instantaneous change. Would Tammy have to transition from being my partner to become my caretaker?

Unbeknownst to her, one of my nurses had experienced what Tammy was going through. A few months before my visit to the E.R., her husband had suffered a stroke. Privately, the nurse prayed that Tammy would not have to go through the same ordeal she had recently experienced.

My parents came to the hospital. My father placed a hand on Tammy's shoulder and offered to stay overnight in the hospital room with me. He knew she needed to go home and rest. Plus the kids were waiting, and luckily being watched by a neighbor.

Tammy cried herself to sleep that night. She didn't know what to expect the following day.

6

"*The search for a scapegoat is*
the easiest of all hunting expeditions."

Dwight D. Eisenhower

Fighting Withdrawals

The Blame Pill

Before the Industrial Age, medicines were hand-mixed. To create pills, a physician would grind the ingredients into a paste. Then he would roll the paste into a tube and cut it into a series of disc shapes. The result was efficient and convenient. Circular pills were easy to swallow and easy to carry without risk of damage.

Similarly, blame uses its form effectively. We learn early on to take the blame pill when in trouble. As toddlers, we figure out how to deflect responsibility to others. When we get away with it, we find relief by avoiding consequences and shame. The next time we sense trouble, we reach for a bottle of blame pills without hesitation.

But there's a problem with this remedy. It's a placebo.

Years ago, when our kids Abbie and Grant were very young, my wife found writing on our daughter's bedroom dresser—ballpoint pen etched deep into the wood. The erratic scribbles couldn't be cleaned off. The dresser was permanently scarred.

Among the inked graffiti on the dresser, a name was inscribed in all caps: G-R-A-N-T. Despite this, my wife did not accuse our son of the crime. Instead, she confronted our 4-year-old daughter Abbie.

She claimed her brother was the culprit. But her pleas fell on deaf ears. The problem with her accusation was her brother's age. He was barely a year old, and could not even write yet.

Abbie received the proper correction for damaging her dresser. In addition, she was given extra consequences for falsely accusing her brother. If our daughter had successfully avoided the blame, how could we have addressed the issue? We couldn't have explained how her actions were destructive—increasing the likelihood she would have attempted to get away with something similar in the future.

This is why blame is a pseudo-remedy. In fact it's actually is worse than a placebo.

Instead of solving a problem, blame enables the development of more problems. Root causes are not addressed while accusers grow addicted to the power they have discovered in a tasty little pill that gets easier to swallow each time you try it again.

Why we perpetuate the cycle

If you ask most people whether blaming others is a good thing, they will likely say it's not. Yet we continue to participate in the epidemic of finger-pointing and scapegoating in today's workplace.

Since we basically understand that blaming others harms our families, businesses, and society at large, why do we keep doing it?

One reason is that many of us don't think it's a problem.

Because of our biases, we don't see how we skirt responsibility and blame others. We imagine ourselves as responsible people who own their mistakes and hold others accountable.

When we're confronted with evidence to the contrary, we damn the messenger. We label the people who see a flaw in our character as irresponsible or jealous—the type of folks who think everything is sour grapes because they didn't get their way.

But if we don't recognize our tendency to blame others, we will never stop our blame habit.

Awareness is an essential step toward a healthier self.

Another reason it's hard to stop blaming others is because the consequences of doing so don't seem to be that serious.

We don't recognize how blaming others negatively impacts them. We don't perceive how it creates a toxic work environment. We see it as part of playing the game to succeed in business. This is reinforced by our belief that the scapegoat deserves the stigma associated with blame.

Finally, we sometimes cling to our blame habit because we need to discharge negative energy.

We discussed earlier that blame could be a tool for dispensing the negativity that builds up after a failure or mistake. If we don't intentionally manage that negative energy with other means, we will continue to rely on blame to defuse the situation.

While it may seem like a solution to release the pressure we sense has built up around us, it can backfire. Arbitrarily discharging our random emotions creates a perpetual culture of blame that escalates negative energy instead of neutralizing it.

"On the shoulders of giants"

Imagine you're on a bike ride on a windy day. You notice when the headwinds are blowing right in your face. You're keenly aware of how much harder you must push the pedals to maintain speed. You feel the wind slowing you down, and you curse it.

Yet, if you turn around, you immediately notice a difference. With the wind at your back, you speed down the path with much less effort. After a while, you forget how much assistance the tailwind provides. You attribute all that extra speed to your effort alone—failing to acknowledge how much the wind supports you.

Studies have shown that we often overestimate our challenges while undervaluing the support we receive. This imbalance is called the Headwinds/Tailwinds Asymmetry. It's a negative cognitive bias that plagues practically every aspect of our lives.

In their study, researchers Shai Davidai and Tom Gilovich found strong evidence of the Headwinds/Tailwinds Asymmetry in a variety of fields. For example, within politics, Democrats and Republicans alike believed the Electoral College worked against their party; while in sports, most fans felt their team specifically had an abnormally difficult schedule; and, in families, siblings each thought they were the ones who were treated most harshly by their parents.

As with a strong headwind, we quickly notice when a person opposes us. We feel how much more difficult it makes things. We pay great attention to how it slows down or stops our progress. We begrudge the 'unfair' burden the opposition places on the circumstance. We may even curse the people standing against us.

The story is much different when the situation is the opposite, and we have people supporting us. We're more likely to downplay how much help we are receiving. We may not acknowledge it or even realize it at all.

This phenomenon doesn't just affect how much credit we give to others or ourselves. It can also affect how much blame we give and receive. If we are acutely aware of resistance to our efforts and ideas, we can blame the people opposing us when a failure occurs.

Contrast this with a statement by mathematician and physicist Sir Isaac Newton, who wrote, "If I have seen further, it is by standing on the shoulders of giants."

Newton recognized that his great accomplishments were made possible by the contributions of many scientists and mathematicians before him. He acknowledged the tailwind pushing him forward.

A match to the tinderbox

In 1980, the average cost of college tuition was less than $10,000 per year. Yet, by 2019, that number had skyrocketed to nearly $30,000—tripling the cost. Meanwhile, the average household income has only increased by 23% when accounting for inflation.

This imbalance spurred much debate as to what caused college tuitions to spiral out-of-control. Some blamed the government for subsidizing the increase with loan programs. Others blamed private lenders who made extensive debt accessible to families who didn't have the financial means to repay the exorbitant costs.

Another group pointed the finger at inflated college athletic budgets used to build colossal stadiums and to pay the multimillion-dollar contracts for coaching staffs. Some also suggested colleges and universities were raising costs to pay for luxurious amenities to attract students to the college experience they wanted.

As tensions escalated, elite universities were able to be highly selective regarding which students they admitted or declined their enrollment. Paying the tuition was not enough. Students had to excel in their classes, perform well on the ACT or SATs, and exhibit leadership skills in their schools and wider community. Prospective students needed exceptional talent to be accepted into specific programs or athletic teams.

The skyrocketing cost of a college education and the exclusivity of elite universities created a tinderbox of stress and anxiety. It would only take a spark to ignite it into a roaring fire of blame.

A hand (or two) in the cookie jar

In the 2010s, William 'Rick' Singer operated a for-profit college preparation business called Edge College & Career Network, known to its customers as The Key. Based in Newport Beach, California, Singer worked with several celebrities across nearly a decade to help their children gain access to premier universities. Bottom line: the bribes supplied by wealthy parents to pay his astronomical fees—approximately $25 million in total.

As the founder and face of the organization, Singer portrayed himself as a fellow parent who sympathized with the pressures put on families to meet exclusive college acceptance requirements.

Tactics used by the staff of The Key included helping students cheat on their entrance exams, falsifying their résumé and school activities, and falsely claiming learning disabilities. Rich parents spared no expense to shoehorn their kids into elite institutions like Yale, Stanford, and USC.

Ultimately, more than 30 parents were charged in the scandal. Among them were actress Felicity Huffman (who won an Emmy for *Desperate Housewives*). In 2019, she pleaded guilty to fraud. For her participation in the scam, Huffman was sentenced to 14 days in federal prison with a year of supervised release. In addition she paid a $30,000 fine and did 250 hours of community service.

Another TV actress Lori Loughlin (best known for *Full House*) and her husband, fashion designer Mossimo Giannulli, were also charged. The couple refused a similar plea agreement and instead decided to plead 'not guilty.'

Unlike Huffman, who had paid merely $15,000 for one child, Loughlin and Giannulli had sunk $500,000 for both daughters to get into the University of Southern California. Fake rowing club profiles were created for the girls, including photos staged on rowing machines, to secure their acceptance as rowing recruits.

The case went to court. While Huffman's case was forgotten, the power couple prolonged their ordeal in the public spotlight.

After a year of fighting the charges, it became clear that the tide had turned on the TV star and her fashion designer husband. The charges against them carried up to 40 years of hard time. So, they changed their plea to 'guilty' and accepted an agreement.

Loughlin served two months in prison, with two years of supervised release, while Giannulli served five months. Their fine was set at $400,000. Denying the allegations and drawing out the case resulted in a more severe penalty than for Felicity Huffman.

Eighteen months later, one of the couple's daughters, Olivia Jade Giannulli, admitted that she did not see why folks were so upset. She assumed most people did something similar to get into college. At the time, she didn't comprehend how the incident highlighted her significant advantages over others her age.

Later, Olivia Jade confessed, "I walked around my whole twenty years of life not realizing, 'You have insane privilege. You're like the poster child of white privilege, and you had no idea.'"

Even if Olivia Jade recognized her tailwind, it seems the scandal created a Headwind/Tailwind Asymmetry for her supporters and critics. The outcry landed on both sides of the issue. While some felt her parents got off easy, others thought the couple were singled out unfairly and treated harshly. The conclusion was an arsenal of blame fired by both sides.

The whole phenomenon of the wealthy and famous fraudulently buying their way into prestigious universities is a vivid example of the Headwind/Tailwind Asymmetry. If they recognized how much support and privilege they had, perhaps they would never have attempted to circumvent the system illegally.

What would change if we all realized the tailwinds helping us throughout each day instead of focusing on the headwinds pushing against us?

Democracy of management

Breaking your blame habit is difficult enough. Changing a blame culture is even more challenging. It's not impossible, but you need to recognize what you're up against.

If you're not at the top of the org chart, one of your biggest challenges may be leadership micromanaging its employees. Under that management style, you may not feel you have the authority to influence the corporate culture. You're more likely to be undermined by leadership when you attempt to make changes.

Interestingly, the term 'micromanage' was not common until the 1980s. Yet, before the concept gained popularity, many experts recognized it as an authoritarian management style. Instead they used words like 'bureaucratic' or 'centralized' management.

Back in 1946, business management guru-to-be Peter Drucker championed a premise he called "democracy of management" in response to the command-and-control style commonly used by managers. At the time, he was working with executives at General Motors to decentralize the car maker's decision-making processes. In a book on the transformation, *The Concept of the Corporation,* he writes about the advantages of this approach:

> *Nobody throws his weight around, yet there is never
> any doubt where the real authority lies. Everybody is free to
> criticize, to talk and to suggest; yet once the decision is
> taken, nobody tries to sabotage it.*

Part of Drucker's aim was to flatten the organization. He wanted to eliminate the huge gap between the 'privileged few' in C-suites and the 'great many' blindly implementing tasks. Everyone should understand and support the corporate objectives rather than relying on 'edict management' (as if those orders were royal decrees).

This strategy, he felt, would create a larger supply of leaders across the company—people invested in their own success as well as GM's. A useful by-product of decentralization is transparency. Weak managers or poor-performing divisions have no place to hide in a structure which can be aggressively critiqued by underlings.

What do you believe about people?

Over a decade later, MIT professor Douglas McGregor proposed two primary management styles. He called them simply Theory X and Theory Y. In his 1960 book, *The Human Side of Enterprise*—which is still considered a touchstone in management literature—McGregor outlined how two distinct beliefs about human nature resulted in two specific approaches to managing people.

Theory X is an Authoritarian Management Style:
- The average person dislikes work—avoiding it if they can
- People must be forced to work under threat of punishment
- People prefer to be directed and to avoid responsibility
- The average person is unambitious, and seeks security

Theory Y is a Participative Management Style:
- Commitment to work is a function of associated rewards
- People will apply self-direction in pursuing objectives
- People usually accept and often seek responsibility
- All people have imagination, ingenuity, and creativity

Battle of the Tech Giants

The management style in an Amazon distribution center is an excellent example of the cynical, authoritarian Theory X.

Workers are watched closely and reprimanded for idle time or looking at their phones. The time it takes to perform everyday tasks, like processing an item, is tracked closely.

If you fall below a threshold early on, a coach will observe you and give you pointers. Later, being too slow results in being written up, which can lead to a productivity firing; this is commonplace. Some workers reported bathroom breaks were discouraged since that might hinder hitting productivity expectations.

Another tech giant, Google, serves as an illustration of the more positive Theory Y management style.

Laszlo Bock, former head of people operations at Google, wrote in his book *Work Rules!* about their approach to managing people. He shared that managers could not make unilateral decisions on whom to hire or fire, performance ratings, raises, promotions, or the final design of a product and when it would launch. Instead, these critical decisions were handled by "a group of peers, a committee, or a dedicated independent team."

Google believes it can get the best output from its people by giving them freedom. They have flexibility with the hours they work and the projects they select. In addition, employees are allowed to spend 20% of their time—roughly one day a week—on personal projects that may not have a direct return on investment.

These corporations are two titans of modern technology, but their management styles are drastically different.

If you are in a Theory X management style culture, blame may be a blunt tool to motivate employees. If so, this compounds the issue. Not only is blame a part of the established culture, but Theory X managers will resist any change that removes the stick they use to manipulate workers into doing their jobs.

The challenges are pretty different in a Theory Y management style culture. With a decentralized model like this, communication can be more complex. A lot of activity happens in silos, which may go unnoticed by managers trying to weed out scapegoating. This structure also makes highlighting positive examples that avoid abusing blame more challenging.

The best place to start is by identifying which theory your work culture leans toward. Then, recognize and plan for the challenges that style will present as you assert to change how you work.

Antibodies and friendly fire

Our mentality is not the only obstacle to overcoming blame. The culture of our environment also creates resistance to change.

Mitra Best, Technology Impact Leader at PWC, calls this corrosive resistance 'corporate antibodies.' She goes on to define it as "the people and processes that extinguish a new idea as soon as it begins to course through the organization."

In biology, antibodies identify any foreign material that enters your body and attack those invaders to protect you from potential harm. This is a critical function of our immune system to eliminate dangerous pathogens, poisons, and other materials from our bodies.

The downside is that this self-defense system works against us. Antibodies have been known to attack the host. More commonly, they attack transplanted organs or body parts since they see the innocent newcomer as a foreign object.

This is why blood type and genetic markers are so crucial to a successful transplant. Unless the transplanted tissue has a nearly identical makeup, the body will attack it and try to reject it.

In business, corporate antibodies work similarly. Unless new employees and their ideas are nearly identical to the existing culture, they will likely be attacked by the established order.

Now you can see why innovation is so challenging for mature organizations. By definition, innovation is new; it involves change. Those are the two primary targets of corporate antibodies. They reject whatever is unique and different from the status quo.

For this reason, companies with strong corporate antibodies find it challenging to reduce the use of blame as a weapon. They also face a double whammy of blame and corporate antibodies hindering their innovation. Not only is it challenging for them to accept new ideas necessary for innovation, but they also foster a culture of fear by accepting and normalizing the practice of blame.

Studies show companies that practice blame are handicapped regarding innovation, creativity, learning, and productivity. If the corporate antibodies win out, the dominant culture doesn't change. The organization loses ground to more innovative competitors who aren't hampered by a fear-driven culture.

It's hard enough for companies to attract and keep talent. A culture of blame makes it even harder to leverage new people, as it prevents these fresh hires from openly sharing their ideas and making significant contributions.

A hostile culture to new talent and ideas makes as much sense as an army bringing in highly skilled recruits—only to fire shots at them. This creates an environment where workers are more focused on the survival of their careers than the purpose of their role at work and the mission of the company.

The court-martial of Billy Mitchell

Changing culture is challenging. This isn't just because of corporate antibodies or a leadership style of micromanaging. It's also because your culture establishes, "This is how we do things around here."

Systems and processes become entrenched because, historically, they seemed to be effective. This reliance on habit creates issues because we no longer live or work in the past. Society and markets—and the millions of undefinable factors they consist of—constantly change. Therefore, "how we do things" should be adapting as well.

Arguably, no institution in contemporary society more strictly adheres to routine and convention than the military.

Over one hundred years ago, at the dawn of the 20th Century, a number of technological innovations were altering society. The first decade saw the introduction of radio, the air conditioner, neon light, the motion picture, and Ford's Model T car. But perhaps none was as transformative as the invention of the airplane.

Humankind had taken flight. And nothing would be the same.

In 1908, a U.S. Army intelligence officer named Billy Mitchell observed the Wright Brothers as they demonstrated one of their flying machines. He was consumed by its potential as an instrument of defense. Mitchell immediately took pilot lessons and urged the military to designate aviation as a separate branch.

By 1916, a year before the United States entered the "war to end all wars" raging in Europe, he was promoted to major and appointed Chief of the Air Service of the First Army.

As World War I continued, it became common for aircraft to be used for surveillance or to engage with other planes in air battles. With America now in the conflict, Mitchell expanded the potential uses of war-time aircraft. He deployed large-scale bombing attacks against the Germans—demonstrating the tactic's effectiveness by sinking a heavily-armored dreadnaught of the Second Reich.

After the war, Mitchell was public with his criticism of the Army's resistance to incorporate aircraft more. After two accidents claimed the lives of several airmen, Mitchell challenged the Army to court martial him. He wanted the nation's attention while making his case for modernizing the country's military air power.

The government obliged. Mitchell got his court martial.

After a two-month trial involving 13 judges (including Major General Douglas McArthur, who found his role in the proceedings "distasteful"), Mitchell was found guilty of broad charges made available under the 96th Article of War. He resigned but continued to promote the advantages of air power as a public citizen.

To influence the culture of the U.S. military, Mitchell had to exhibit the courage to stand up to leaders, including President Calvin Coolidge. It resulted in ending his promising military career.

Today, Billy Mitchell is considered to be the father of the United States Air Force, which was founded 22 years after his court martial. He also predicted the Japanese attack on Pearl Harbor 17 years before it occurred. He is memorialized as the first American to have an aircraft named after them (the North American B-25 Mitchell) as well as the Milwaukee Mitchell International Airport in Wisconsin.

Not a bad legacy for trying to bend an inflexible culture.

Even if you work in a collaborative office, breaking the path dependency created over the years, decades, or even centuries can be challenging. When you try to change anything—from how we hold meetings to how successes and failures are handled—you're likely to meet with the phrase, "That's not how we do things around here."

This doesn't necessarily mean you should invite a court martial.

But don't be surprised by resistance and possible attack.

Covering your ass

Even if you don't encounter a direct attack on your position, you need to be prepared for the office defense used by tons of workers—covering your ass. CYA is a time-worn tactic of habitual blamers.

To elaborate on this more deeply, let's return to the case of Amanda Knox. During the initial investigation of the murder of her roommate Meredith Kercher, authorities brought in three people for questioning as 'persons of interest'—Knox; her boyfriend, Raffaele Sollecito; and her boss, Patrick Lumumba (a bar owner).

At one point, Amanda claimed she saw Lumumba standing over the dead body of Kercher. He not only denied the claim but was able to provide an alibi that led to his release.

Knox later alleged police coerced her to accuse Lumumba of the murder. She stated that officers had pressured her and even struck her on the back of her head when she gave answers they didn't like. Under duress and exhaustion, she blamed Lumumba because she accepted what the police told her. It became a false memory.

Another eventual suspect in the case, Rudy Guede—a 20-year-old Ivory Coast immigrant who lived nearby—accused Amanda of committing the crime.

Before his arrest, Guede was recorded via a Skype call with a friend saying Knox had nothing to do with the murder and was not even at the crime scene when it occurred. With evidence mounting against him, Guede changed his story multiple times. He reverted to claiming Amanda was the one who actually killed Kercher.

In both of these cases, the suspects blamed others when they experienced intense emotional strain. Based on the evidence, it was apparent Guede lied many times. But Amanda was also inconsistent. By applying pressure, the authorities trapped both suspects in a metaphorical corner.

While the Kercher murder was a sensational story, the reasons that both suspects blamed others are relatively common. They both looked to escape the tremendous stress of their situation. Each felt their only possible outlet was to blame someone else. Both of them lied because they were afraid.

None of these characteristics are unusual in the workplace.

Every person experiences pressure, confusion, and fatigue at work. Perhaps we try to alleviate it by using blame avoidance, scapegoating, or outright lying. Workplaces are full of unrealistic expectations and hustle cultures that burn people out. That's why Cover Your Ass is a well-known acronym (CYA).

It seems that toxic workplaces have a lot in common with poorly run police investigations. The wrong people get blamed, while true culprits run free. Injustice becomes the air we breath.

Suppose we, like the Italian investigators who falsely accused Amanda Knox, ignore the evidence and pursue our biases and gut instincts. In that case, we would be guilty of spreading and inflicting an injustice upon others.

What are the alternatives?

PART 3

Blaming
Ourselves

7

"It must be due to some fault in ourselves.
The solution, as I see it, is to work harder. From now
onwards, I shall get up a full hour earlier in the mornings."

Boxer in George Orwell's *Animal Farm*

Consequences
of Self-Blame

Taking one for the team

Blaming others is one way to avoid being held accountable. But, doing the exact opposite—blaming yourself—does not instantly create accountability.

When we blame others, we see them as hindering us from accomplishing our goals. We believe we could fulfill our potential if only other people weren't in the way, always holding us back. We use this kind of blame as an excuse to justify underperforming. This effectively makes others "responsible for your misery," as Rabbi Harold Kushner phrased it.

While blaming others may be alluring because it allows us to avoid personal responsibility and accountability, most of us still recognize that blame-shifting is a negative character trait. We tend to lose respect for people who continually fault others for their own mistakes. We also would not want to be characterized as someone who habitually blames others.

At the same time, there is something almost admirable about being the person who takes the blame. Like a baseball player who lets a pitch hit them while at bat or a soldier willing to take a bullet for his fellow man. The problem with these analogies is the soldier sacrifices to save others' lives, while the batter 'takes one for the team' to put a runner on base.

Taking blame does not similarly help others.
In fact, it can be detrimental.

Conditioned for Self-Loathing

Blaming ourselves can stunt our growth just as severely, sometimes worse, than blaming others. It leads us to believe we are the primary reason for any failure. We then identify with failure itself.

This is odd because we are selective with this phenomenon. As mentioned in Chapter 1—if you consider yourself a runner, on the day you fall, you don't suddenly start calling yourself a "faller." Yet we often do this when we fail at work.

A project manager with dozens of successful projects under her belt falls into the trap of believing she is a failure after a single project falls short of its goals. This self-limiting belief can cause her to second-guess her abilities and even stall out her career. Identifying with failure is a form of self-blame. Instead of seeing the problem we are caught within, we think we're the problem.

Conflating our identity with our circumstances compounds our situation. Instead of changing our circumstances to create a solution, we believe the issue is part of our character. We ignore the actual problem while simultaneously damaging our self-image. Even if we identify a real solution, we may not feel we can achieve it due to the flaws we have attributed to our character.

When self-blame becomes part of our identity, it's hard to break the cycle.

Drawing on the back of the worksheet

Growing up, I was not a physically-active kid. I liked to read and spent hours drawing pictures. I preferred this over anything I found physically taxing. The adults in my life saw this as a sign of laziness.

I remember turning in a worksheet to my teacher in third grade. Mrs. Buchanan looked at the blank sheet and asked why I didn't do my work. I proudly told her I was making art the entire class period. She turned over the paper to see it was full of colorful drawings. Shortly after this incident, Mrs. Buchanan transferred me to another teacher, citing a "personality conflict" between the two of us.

She wasn't being malicious. It's just that Mrs. Buchanan found me challenging to motivate. So did my coaches when I played team sports. They only wanted to help our team develop character and be competitive on the field. All of these adults were good people.

This applies to my folks as well. My family heritage is German, thus my parents are the type of people who get things done instead of waiting around. They tried to instill a healthy work ethic in me. But as an impressionable young child, I took their criticism to heart and assumed it was part of my identity.

We all had some less-than-desirable characteristics as a child, which caring adults probably tried to address. More than likely, their focus on correction was well-intended, but it could also reinforce a negative image of ourselves.

Although it's never set in stone, our self-image is mainly formed by the time we reach our teens. This means that we establish much of our perception of ourselves long before we fully develop mentally. Also, we create this perception when we are immature and less capable of nuanced thinking.

As a result, when we blame ourselves, our self-image may be completely inaccurate, but it's hard to shake an identity that has been ingrained in us. Accepting unfair blame creates self-loathing, which makes us even more susceptible to self-blame in the future.

Carving our negatives in stone

To this day, I struggle with seeing myself as lazy. I feel guilty when a project goes awry, and my first reaction is to criticize myself for not doing enough. I see that flawed eight-year-old small-town boy who shirked his chores in favor of creating a fantasy land using his colored pencils and watercolors.

My fixation on perceived character flaws makes it too easy to accept blame when any issue arises that I can blame on laziness. And if I'm tying that blame and failure to my identity, then I won't see opportunities to fix the issue or to learn from it and grow—so I can do better next time.

In her wildly popular book *Mindset: The Psychology of Success*, Stanford psychologist Carol Dweck states it this way:

Believing that your qualities are carved in stone—the fixed mindset—creates an urgency to prove yourself over and over.

According to Dweck, a fixed mindset causes us to engage in negative bias. We avoid challenges; we give up easily; we ignore useful negative feedback; and we feel threatened by others' success.

Additionally, researchers have shown that self-blame is both a cause and a symptom of deeper issues like depression, anxiety, and self-doubt. Allowing our failures to shape our identity and establish a fixed mindset—where we see no potential for growth—is dangerous for our mental health.

When we criticize someone with name-calling, we attack that person's identity. We create the conditions for self-loathing. If we call someone 'lazy' enough times, they may start believing it's part of who they are—instead of a behavior they tend to do.

This isn't just an issue for individuals; it also contributes to systemic problems in the workplace. Flaws in an organization's processes, tools, or skills are left unaddressed when we assume the company's fixed identity is the root cause.

The double-edged sword of positivity

A wealth of religious and self-help movements focus on the power of positive thinking. From the most popular minister among the Silent Generation, Norman Vincent Peale, and his book *The Power of Positive Thinking*, to the world-famous media icon, Oprah Winfrey, endorsing the new age book and movie *The Secret*.

Focusing on positive thoughts and words broadly appeals to religious and pop culture groups. For some reason, we want to believe this philosophy will fulfill its promise of increasing the number of good things happening in our daily lives. On the surface, this seems like a helpful harmless exercise.

But what if the opposite is true?

In her *New York Times* bestselling book *Bright-Sided: How the Relentless Promotion of Positive Thinking Has Undermined America*, author Barbara Ehrenreich points out the unintended consequences resulting from the philosophy of positive thinking:

The flip side of positivity is thus a harsh insistence on personal responsibility: if your business fails or your job is eliminated, it must be because you didn't try hard enough, didn't believe firmly enough in the inevitability of your success.

How ironic is that? If you don't get exactly what you want, it's your fault. On its surface, positive thinking is constructive and full of optimism, but Ehrenreich shows us the other side of the coin:

There is the darker message that if you don't have all that you want, if you feel sick, discouraged, or defeated, you have only yourself to blame.

The pressure to be positive creates the opposite of its intended effect—negativity. In *Bright-Sided*, the author mentions the weight of failing to think positively could be like a second disease for cancer patients. She shared this from her personal experience as she battled breast cancer. I saw something similar occur in my church.

The Stockdale Paradox

Growing up, my family was part of the Word of Faith movement founded by evangelist Kenneth Hagin. Members of such churches didn't dare admit they were struggling financially, physically, or otherwise. Churchgoers were told to claim what they wanted.

Accepting they were in a bad situation was considered a lack of faith. If anyone voiced their worries, it could bring their maladies into existence. Critics called this movement "Name it. Claim it."

In a way, the teachings were a form of self-fulfilling prophecy. If you stuck to proclaiming everything was fabulous, that must be your reality. If you broke down and divulged things weren't that great, then your faithless confession caused your misfortune.

But this approach doesn't allow us to deal with reality. It discourages us from facing the facts and repaints them into beautiful fiction. The consequences of this mindset can be dire. In his seminal bestselling business book *Good to Great*, author Jim Collins shared a conversation between him and former Vice Presidential candidate James Stockdale—a prisoner of war during the Vietnam War.

When Collins asked the former POW to describe who didn't make it out of Vietnam, he was surprised by Stockdale's response. It turned out the optimists didn't make it.

The Navy veteran explained that these were the soldiers who said they'd be out by Christmas. When that didn't happen, they'd channel their positivity into being out by Easter. Easter would come and go, as would Thanksgiving. Then another Christmas.

Stockdale conjectured that they "died of a broken heart."

Collins coined this ironic maxim the Stockdale Paradox. You must maintain a hope that you will prevail while still confronting the brutal facts of your reality.

It is not healthy to deny our reality. Accepting the philosophy of positive thinking takes anything negative that occurs in our lives and places it at our own feet. It encourages self-blame.

Painted ourselves into a corner

Yet, the basis of positive thinking was not restricted to religion, medicine, or the battlefield. Ehrenreich claimed it has also found itself quite comfortable in the confines of our workplaces.

> *Nowhere did [positive thinking] find a warmer welcome than in American business, which is… also global business.*

It was welcomed by employees who wanted to enjoy the third of of their waking lives spent at work. Employers saw it as a way to prod their workers to put in more hours and be more productive.

Ehrenreich suggests it was a "liberating ideology" for executives to help them cope with their ever-increasing stress. They found relief in the idea that good things come to those who think positively. Like the optimistic POWs, they denied their reality and clung to a false promise that things would improve if they only claimed they would.

We paint ourselves into a corner by avoiding the brutal reality and pinning our hopes on our own ability to spin. We neglect the pursuit of real solutions, which increases the likelihood of failure. Then, we are left to either continue rejecting the facts or blame ourselves for not willing success into existence.

We create a binary choice of becoming a charlatan or a failure.

The Spotlight Effect

Barry Manilow is one of the top-selling music artists of all time. He's sold more than 85 million albums worldwide over his career.

Now in his late 70s, he still does limited tours while performing more than 60 times a year at the Westgate Resort in Las Vegas. Manilow has reached the 'sequin Elvis' stage of his career. His fans are so dedicated they have their own nickname—"Fanilows."

Yet, while diehard believers consider him "the showman of our generation," others call him "the king of schmaltz." Thus, in 2000, when Cornell psychology professor Thomas Gilovich and his team wanted to make college students feel self-conscious—they decided to have them wear a Barry Manilow t-shirt.

As part of a research study, Gilovich asked the students to wear a Manilow-emblazoned shirt, then walk into a roomful of strangers. Later, the researchers asked the participants what percentage of the room they thought had noticed their sartorial faux pas. On average, the students guessed that half the strangers recalled the shirt. The truth, however, was closer to twenty percent.

Gilovich dubbed this phenomenon 'the spotlight effect.'

The research team concluded that others are not as aware of our shortcomings as we believe they are. Gilovich's earlier research had shown that individuals commonly regretted not taking the initiative because of concerns about how a potential failure would look to others. Combining these results, the team hypothesized we'd have fewer regrets if we realized how little attention our flaws and errors receive from others.

Bottom line: we should take more chances.

Everyone is at the center of the world

Like others, I have struggled with the spotlight effect during my life. Even today, when an embarrassing memory comes to mind, I think about what I did and who was present to witness it, and I experience the shame all over again.

I don't feel this way simply because of what I did, but mostly because I imagine that—just as I am obsessing about it—those who saw my blunder continue to think about how stupid I was.

The reality is that they're probably too busy remembering the awkward things they've done even to consider my foolishness.

Years ago, to help me overcome my self-consciousness, I printed a quote from the 1930s-era jokesmith Olin Miller and posted it on the wall of my office. I placed it at eye level, next to my computer monitor, so that I would see it often.

> *You probably wouldn't worry about what people think of you if you could know how seldom they do.*

This reminded me that I couldn't let the spotlight effect control my decision-making. Recognizing that as Abraham Lincoln said at Gettysburg, "the world will little note nor long remember," helps me to make choices based on my convictions and beliefs instead of succumbing to my fear of others' judgment.

The same is true for mistakes, issues, and failures at work. If we use limited information to identify who to blame, the spotlight effect can easily trick us into believing we deserve to be a scapegoat.

Feeling this way because of a Barry Manilow t-shirt can seem silly. But what if the situation was drastically more severe?

A decision on the bridge

As the clouds parted on a chilly Saturday morning in February 2017, a thoracic surgeon leapt from the side of the George Washington Bridge that spans the Hudson River between New York and New Jersey. He plunged 200 feet—dying on impact with the water.

A few hours later, a phone rang at the home of another doctor in nearby Fort Lee, the borough connected to Manhattan by the GW Bridge. The woman who picked up was Jennifer Ashton, the Chief Medical Correspondent for ABC News. On the other end was her doorman announcing the arrival of three detectives. As a matter of fact, they were already on their way up to her apartment.

Jennifer had just stepped out of the shower to take the call. She was caught off guard by the news that police officers were about to walk in. Her mind raced. Perhaps this was related to an illegal u-turn she'd made the night before, which resulted in a ticket. But why such a show of force for a simple traffic violation?

After quickly putting on some clothes, Jennifer answered the door. The men identified themselves as Port Authority Police. Suddenly, she knew this was much bigger.

She invited the three men to come in and sit down. The lead detective sat on the ottoman directly in front of her and explained, "Dr. Ashton, we found a piece of paper with your name and number and the words 'call my wife' on the remains of your husband."

Jennifer inhaled deeply to calm herself.

In truth, the man who jumped off the bridge to end his life was no longer her husband. They'd divorced just eighteen days before his death. Jennifer later confessed to her brother that it was all her fault. In an interview years later, she explained her feelings.

"I blamed myself for not seeing potential signs, even though there were none. And I blamed myself for what I perceived as a failure to protect my children from pain, that they had to live through this."

The mother of two also blamed herself for not being the one who gave her daughter Chloe the life-altering news that her father had died. Chloe was attending a private school an hour away. Still in shock, Jennifer asked her brother and son to drive to Lawrenceville private boarding school without her.

Through counseling and the support of friends and family, Jennifer realized her ex-husband's suicide and its repercussions on her family were not her fault. The divorce was amicable. Robert had no diagnosis of depression, and there were no warning signs of suicidal tendencies. His suicide caught everyone off-guard.

But blame is a typical response when a loved one commits suicide. Research has shown those who experience a suicide loss are more likely to self-blame than others who lose someone to natural causes. They are also considered to have a higher risk of committing suicide themselves.

Just because she was a medical and media success story didn't make Dr. Ashton an exception to self-blame. In fact, her situation compounded the blame.

Robert Ashton's suicide note started with the line, "First of all, this is no one's fault." But she found no comfort in those words.

Jennifer's brother emphasized she was not at fault, that no one saw this coming. But the predatory media coverage, searching for an angle, insinuated otherwise. Since the divorce and suicide were separated by less than three weeks, it was irresistible as a headline.

Articles announced, "Top surgeon jumps to his death following divorce from TV personality," reinforcing Jennifer's struggle with self-blame. Note that people who are susceptible to self-blame are at even greater risk in a world that stokes the fires of blame culture.

Jennifer sought help from her therapist. Eventually, she shared her story with others. She listened with empathy to people who had suffered the loss of a loved one from suicide. All of this contributed to her understanding she wasn't to blame for her ex-husband's death.

Seeking help

All too often the shame and isolation created by blame discourages us from seeking help, sharing our story, or talking with others who have experienced similar struggles.

This seems like an appropriate place to mention that if you struggle with depression or thoughts of suicide, I encourage you to follow Jennifer Ashton's model and seek help. Silence and isolation are not answers.

There is hope.

In the United States, you can call or text three simple digits (988) to connect to the 988 Suicide and Crisis Lifeline—a network of more than two hundred crisis centers that helps people overcome crisis situations every single day. They provide confidential support to anyone in suicidal crisis or mental health-related distress.

8

"*Our greatest fear is fear of success. When we are succeeding—
that is, when we have begun to overcome our self-doubt and
self-sabotage, when we are advancing in our craft and evolving
to a higher level—that's when panic strikes.*"

Steven Pressfield, *Do the Work*

Creating our own Obstacles

The art of self-sabotage

There's a plot device found in multiple sci-fi movies when the heroes are about to be vanquished. They have exhausted all options. The enemy has overwhelmed them. Their weapons are depleted. Their defenses are down. The enemy is boarding the ship.

All hope is lost.

The captain of the ship then gives the command. "Activate auto-destruct sequence." He provides the authorization code, and we hear the computer count down to its own obliteration.

Sometimes something miraculous happens. The heroes identify a path to victory and disable the sequence. Sometimes the ship detonates, but the crew narrowly escapes. The invading enemy may be destroyed, or some powerful weapon or secret is kept out of their evil clutches. Then, there are versions where the captain has to stay on board to ensure the rest of the crew can leave safely. He sacrifices himself to save the lives of his people.

The common theme in these scenarios is that all hope was lost because there was no alternative.

Often when things become uncomfortable, we're programmed to activate an auto-destruct sequence. The catch is that we don't wait until we have depleted all other options.

It is our default setting.

Too much stress? "Activate auto-destruct sequence."

On the brink of failure? "Activate auto-destruct sequence."

On the verge of success? "Activate auto-destruct sequence."

Why would we self-destruct when success is possible? The stress of teetering between failure and success can make us feel like we are losing control and the results are uncertain. As counterintuitive as it seems, self-destruction fixes that issue. We know where blowing up the ship will take us, to a familiar place—guaranteed failure.

We'd rather control our failure than accept uncertain success.

This condition is similar to a sensation experienced over and over again by gambling addicts. When researchers studied the brain activity of gamblers, they found something interesting. The chemical reaction when gamblers won a bet was practically identical to when they *almost* won. This is called the near-miss effect.

Addicted to the slots

Casinos understand this tendency. Thus, most gambling games are configured so the player will come close enough to winning that they stay addicted to playing, enjoying another near-miss.

If the slot machine shows two cherries, then the last image may be a strawberry. It's a red fruit. It's so close you can almost envision the three cherries and the resulting jackpot. Or at the roulette table, a spinning wheel slows down as it crosses over a big prize, making the player believe they almost won a windfall.

Addicted players don't realize they're no longer playing to win. They're playing to almost win. In reality, they're chasing a dopamine hit. Since near misses provide that chemical rush, they're not just addicted to gambling—they're addicted to losing.

Self-destructors are similar to gambling addicts.

We can feel like the system is rigged against us, that we'll never win. In a way, we're right. It's not some cruel twist of fate, and it isn't just because of the system. It's because we've been conditioned to venture after something other than success.

In the same way gamblers chase near misses, self-destructors pursue near successes. When results hang in the balance, there's a seductive tension. Failure at the mercy of others—a boss, a client, the market—can be painful feedback that makes you feel insufficient.

Yet, failure on your own terms means you are choosing to quit. You can rationalize—thinking you might've been successful if you'd decided to continue. Maybe you even convince yourself that you didn't want to win in the first place. The sense of control and relief we gain after resigning to failure fools us into believing we won.

But technically, 'almost winning' is just another way of saying 'losing.' And self-blame is another way of self-destructing.

The fiction of confessions

All this talk of self-destruction returns us again to the ongoing saga of Amanda Knox and the murder of Meredith Kercher.

Based on what we discussed in previously, it seems like the truth is clear. Amanda did not kill her roommate. Instead, Rudy Guede was guilty of the heinous crime. But, if you search online and delve into message threads on sites like Reddit, you'll find many folks who still believe Knox participated somehow. These opinions are based heavily on one fact—Amanda confessed.

If Knox were innocent, why in the world would she confess to committing murder? Surely only a guilty person would do this.

Saul Kassin disagrees. He believes Amanda Knox gave a false confession. Kassin is a Professor of Psychology at John Jay College of Criminal Justice, and he wrote the book on psychology. In fact, he has written 13 different books on psychology and criminal justice. He's considered an expert in interrogations and confessions.

According to Professor Kassin, there are three categories of false confessions: voluntary, compliant, and internalized. The distinctions might seem a little academic, so let's break them down one-by-one.

Voluntary false confessions typically occur in high-profile cases where people can gain public attention. As an example, think of the kidnapping of aviator Charles Lindbergh's infant son in 1932. More than 200 people confessed to the crime. Yet none of them were the person eventually found guilty.

In fact, voluntary false confessions often come from individuals with delusions or mental health issues. This category also includes some who confess to a crime they didn't commit to protect someone they feared would otherwise be blamed.

A crime in Central Park

Kassin's second category, compliant false confessions, occurs when individuals know they're innocent but confess to escape a situation they feel is worse than not confessing. You may recall the Central Park jogger case in 1989. A group of five teenage boys were accused of raping and nearly killing a woman at night in New York's largest city park. All five were convicted the next year.

The case's linchpin had been that the young men confessed after intense interrogations. Each of them claimed they expected to go home afterward. They saw confession as their only way out of the harsh questioning, but instead, this was used to convict them.

The youths, aged 14 to 16, when the crime was committed were sentenced to prison. But this was not enough for many in the public, who'd been whipped into a frenzy by the salacious media coverage of the case. Many called for politicians to reinstate the death penalty. The most famous among them being Manhattan real estate tycoon Donald Trump. He spent $85,000 (equal to over $200,000 today) to run full-page ads in New York City's four largest newspapers stating "Bring back the death penalty." This threw gas on the fire. As a result of the ads, a family of the accused received multiple death threats.

Ultimately, the four youngest of the accused served from 6 to 7 years, while the oldest, Korey Wise, was incarcerated over 13 years. In fact, Wise actually met the real rapist face-to-face in 2001 while both were in prison. It's thought that this chance encounter is what caused the actual criminal to finally confess to the crime. A fact which was confirmed by DNA evidence.

Today the five innocent men are known as the Exonerated Five.

Believing you did the crime

The final category on Kassin's list is internalized false confessions. This involves an innocent person who is coerced—either by their vulnerability, like a mental impairment, or by subjection to extreme interrogation tactics—into confessing to a crime while internally believing they actually committed the act in question.

This can occur when the suspect, under incredible stress from the death of someone close to them, submits to the pressure of the authorities accusing them of the murder. The police can compound the situation by lying about evidence and events, which confuses the suspect and causes them to doubt their own reality. Kassin says these individuals eventually confess by using words like, "I guess I did it" or "I guess I must have done it."

As you may have guessed, a textbook example of an internalized false confession is Amanda Knox's admission of guilt. Of that time period, she said:

> I was scared; I was confused; I'd been with the police for hours. I thought they were protecting me, but instead, they were putting me under pressure; they were threatening me.

The police interpreter and a detective testified that Amanda appeared tired and exhausted even before she was questioned. Then the police interrogated her day and night. By the time she signed her confession, Amanda had been with the police for over 53 hours. She could not speak Italian very well, so there were several moments of misunderstanding, adding to her confusion.

Amanda stated that, at times, the police yelled at her. She claimed they struck her on the back of the head. Later, she told the TV news show *Nightline* the police had said she had amnesia.

> And so what they were forcing me to consider was that my memories that I had—that I had spent the night with Raffaele—were wrong and that I needed to re-scramble my brain around to bring out the truth.

False confessions at work

If people can be confused and manipulated into accepting that they're guilty of a murder they didn't commit, how much easier is it to accept the blame when our business loses an important account, or when we don't get the job we interviewed for, or when a sales pitch to major new customer falls flat?

Plenty of work environments put us in stressful situations and ask us to work long hours, sometimes to the point of fatigue. Some leaders can act like prosecutors interrogating a suspect when they question the performance of an employee.

I can see all three types of false confession occurring as self-blame in the workplace. Do you recognize theses as well?

Voluntary self-blame: A person knows they aren't to blame but either wants attention or wants to protect someone else.

Compliant self-blame: This person doesn't believe they're to blame but are only accepting it to get out of a bad situation.

Internalized self-blame: Someone is coerced into believing they are to blame because of confusion, stress, and pressure.

Before you accept the blame for something or decide to let someone else volunteer to be a scapegoat, ask whether this is a 'false confession' instead.

Fear and self-loathing in Las Vegas

When you grow up, you'll discover that you have defended lies, deceived yourself, or suffered foolishness. If you're a good warrior you will not blame yourself for this, but neither will you allow your mistakes to repeat themselves.

Paulo Coelho

As we discuss self-blame, you may be feeling some tension. Maybe you wonder if there are things you should blame yourself for. You don't want to let yourself off the hook or shirk your responsibilities.

Don't worry. That's not what we're talking about here. Responsibility is owning your actions, but it doesn't mean taking ownership of another person's actions. Accountability is allowing others to hold you subject to your commitments. You take on responsibility, knowing you may be held accountable later.

Actions have consequences, and short-circuiting the course of those natural events hampers the growth of individuals and the health of our society. When we continually rescue our children from the consequences of their own decisions, we shouldn't be surprised to discover them lacking maturity and discipline (I realize there are exceptions, but this should not be the rule). There are many valid and necessary reasons why we should continue to hold ourselves and others accountable for what we say and do.

Simultaneously, the pendulum shouldn't swing too far the other way. Just as we mustn't shirk responsibility, it's equally important we do not mistakenly believe we can use blame as a substitute for it.

This doesn't work primarily because blame is not synonymous with responsibility or accountability. Blame is the resentment we feel toward those we hold at fault. Let me say that again.

Blame is resentment.

Holding onto resentment, as I quoted Susan Cheever earlier, "is like taking poison and waiting for the other person to die." In the case of self-blame, it's like resenting yourself. When you view it in this light, you can see how this habit can lead to unhealthy outcomes.

Self-blame is a roadblock

A recent survey by the Canadian Lung Association showed a high percentage of lung cancer patients also suffer from self-blame. The association's CEO, Terry Dean, stated that even though lung disease can affect anyone, its stigma ranges from misrepresentation and misinformation to blame and judgment.

Educating the public on the increased risk of lung cancer for smokers has helped prevent many from such dire consequences. At the same time, these campaigns have also had adverse side effects.

The public knowledge that smoking can lead to lung disease has had the unfortunate side effect of people often getting blamed for their disease if they have smoked.

A significant number of people with lung cancer (42%) reported feeling less deserving of help than those with other forms of cancer. Because lung cancer is considered mostly preventable by avoiding smoking, these patients felt they had brought the disease upon themselves. Most other forms of cancer didn't have such an emphasis on a stigmatized, unhealthy habit like smoking.

Related to their low sense of worthiness for treatment, 45% of all lung cancer patients said they put off going to the doctor because of self-blame. Interestingly, this number is even higher than those who felt less deserving of help. Delaying necessary doctor appointments increases the chance of complications regarding treatment. So, not only is self-blame not an effective answer, but it also works against the potential solutions offered by treatment.

Self-blame at work can have similar effects.

When we blame negative events and outcomes on ourselves, it likely decreases our sense of self-worth. We lower our expectations of ourselves and what we can achieve. When we struggle, we won't see ourselves as deserving of help, so we are less likely to seek the help of teammates and leaders. We are also less likely to strive to achieve our personal and organizational goals.

All of this can exacerbate the negative situations we are already in and work against finding a solution for those issues—increasing the likelihood of similar negative events and outcomes reoccurring.

The loss of perfection

Self-blame is especially prevalent among women in the workforce. British business researchers Dr. Darren T. Baker and Deborah N. Brewis studied gender equality in the workplace. Along with work by business school professor Dr. Juliet Bourke at the University of New South Wales, their research identified a pattern of self-blaming by women when they don't live up to their idealized work standards. Because they are not the perfect worker, these women felt they're to blame for any shortcomings they experience in their careers.

In Baker and Bourke's *Harvard Business Review* article, "How Confidence Is Weaponized Against Women," they challenge the recent flurry of advice given to businesswomen with regards to demonstrating self-confidence.

Women are constantly told to 'lean in' to achieve their career goals. Be a 'girl boss.' They're encouraged to use body language, eye contact, and vocal inflections to make an impression. And no matter what, they are told to 'fake it till you make it.' Somehow, they are expected to do all this while appearing approachable and likable.

The research revealed that women found their self-confidence (or lack thereof) as a significant contributor to their own career progression and that of other women. On the other hand, men did not see self-confidence as an aid or impediment to their careers nor the careers of their male colleagues.

While the findings showed that women's confidence had some benefits, it also highlighted these benefits were only temporary. Even when they were mistreated, these women tended to take the blame for the situation. They regretted not seizing opportunities or 'putting themselves out there' more. They blamed themselves for stagnant careers. This was a way of constructing an alternative reality that their ambitions could only be realized with greater self-confidence.

Similar to the philosophy of positive thinking we discussed before, this cult of self-confidence causes individuals to double down on their faulty premise. If having self-confidence didn't get a woman that promotion, she then believes she must not have demonstrated enough confidence. Like the dedicated but dim-witted horse Boxer in Orwell's *Animal Farm*, she tells herself, "I will work harder."

In their *HBR* article, researchers Brown and Bourke revealed how this perfectionism was faulty in its logic. It denied women an opportunity to be vulnerable and humble. This lack of humanization is also detrimental to workplace psychological safety. It damages others' ability to relate to us.

In line with other instances of blame, the research found that women who focused on self-blame often ignored systemic barriers to their ambitions. It distracted them from addressing any unfair work practices holding them back. Just as Boxer ignored his fate even as he was loaded onto the cart to go to the glue factory.

Once again, the siren call of blame—even self-blame—distracts us from solutions.

9

"*Suffering is part of life, and we don't have to feel it's happening because we personally made the wrong move.*"

Pema Chödrön, *When Things Fall Apart*

Identity and Self-Blame

9

Hairballs and geniuses

The late Gordon MacKenzie was a creative force at Hallmark Cards in the '80s and '90s. With his white hair and goatee, combined with his round glasses, MacKenzie looked like Merlin from the Arthurian Knights of the Round Table. And, in his own way, he was a wizard.

Always wanting to inspire creativity in other people, this artistic wizard visited schools in the Kansas City area. He showed students his sculptures and talked about the life of an artist. Each time he'd start by asking the students if they considered themselves artists.

Since MacKenzie visited a spectrum of grade levels, he noticed a disturbing trend occurring as he asked this question.

In kindergarten, all the hands in the room went up. Each little child excitedly thrust both arms high into the air. But, just one year later, when he asked first graders the same question, only about half as many hands were raised.

This attrition continued as the age groups progressed until, by sixth grade, hardly anyone raised a hand. Those who did darted their eyes back and forth, sensing they were outing themselves as artists to a roomful of apostates.

Then Gordon asked, "What happened to all the artists? Did they transfer to art school?" The kids would laugh nervously. They got the joke. Gordon answered for them. "I'm afraid it's something more sinister than that. You've been tricked out of the greatest gift we're all given at birth—your identity as a creative genius."

Then the wizard worked his magic. He reconnected kids to their artistic identity. He explained how each of us contains a masterpiece inside. If we do not create it, no one would. MacKenzie opened eyes to see how the world tries to suppress creative genius. He sparked a hope in his students for them to regain their identity—and keep it.

Similarly, MacKenzie helped adults reconnect with their creative genius through his workshops and magnum opus book, *Orbiting the Giant Hairball*. He excelled at encouraging people to survive the "corporate normalcy" without sacrificing their artistic identity. In fact, while at Hallmark, MacKenzie fashioned his own title: Creative Paradox. He explains, "My job was to be loyally subversive." Sort of a court jester among all the grey suits.

Gordon listed a number of creative geniuses opposed by society: folks like Galileo, Socrates, Joan of Arc, and Jesus of Nazareth. He admits that the societies those people lived in didn't always intend to suppress true genius. Often, they wanted to eliminate what they thought was foolishness that might unravel their way of life. They wanted these luminaries to 'be normal' because their abnormalities threatened the authority of those in control.

A primary tool societies use in their deceptive theft of artistic identity is blame.

Nudging and shoving

The blame game starts early. We pressure our young kids to grow up, to leave 'silly notions' of creativity and imagination behind.

"You don't really want to be an artist when you're older. How will you make any money?"

Children are discouraged from harboring fanciful ideas while being nudged (or shoved) towards the acceptable status quo that will give them a competitive advantage.

Why?

Because if they aren't successful, who will get blamed?

Parents are afraid of being blamed for being too lax. Teachers don't want to be blamed for giving impractical advice to students. The kids don't want to be blamed for disappointing either of them.

Gordon reminded those kids—and each of us—that we are all creative geniuses. It's our birthright. It isn't something to be ashamed of. It isn't blameworthy. It should be a source of pride. It isn't about being a starving artist or a successful engineer. It's more than that.

Maintaining our identity is a critical component of avoiding self-blame.

Observing our independence

Spiritual teacher and author Eckhart Tolle has reached millions with his books and teachings. In fact, the *New York Times* dubbed him, "the most popular spiritual author in the United States."

Yet, when he was 29, Tolle struggled deeply with his life. So much so that he was ready to end it. In the midst of depression, he awoke early one morning and felt a powerful sense of dread. There, alone in the darkness, he loathed everything—even himself.

Then he had a realization.

> *If I cannot live with myself, there must be two of me: the 'I' and the 'self' that 'I' cannot live with. Maybe, I thought, only one of them is real.*

Eckhart Tolle, *The Power of Now*

After his epiphany, Tolle vividly described a seemingly metaphysical transformation he experienced. It changed how he viewed himself and everything around him. Everything became beautiful and alive. All because he recognized he had two identities.

In line with Tolle's catalytic experience, psychologist Rollo May claimed, "The human dilemma is that which arises out of a man's capacity to experience himself as both subject and object at the same time." He argued that one needs to be both 'the observer' and 'the observed' to have a meaningful life.

Unfortunately, we are outstanding observers. Our consumer society has trained us to be the audience, watching hours of TV and movies. Even our participation in video games has given way to our desire to watch others play video games on the streaming service Twitch. In just a generation, we've gone from activity to interactivity to passively observing someone else's interactivity.

Yet there are other times when we disregard our ability to observe and solely become the observed instead.

Self-blame disregards our ability to change and grow. Instead of understanding why we made a mistake, we accept criticism and blame from others. We fault our flawed personality, bad luck, inferior intelligence, or some other inextricable characteristic.

Thus we avoid a deeper inspection of our essential self. It seems as though blaming yourself results from too much self-reflection. It's more likely that we're failing to peel back enough layers to separate ourselves from learned behaviors that can be changed.

Examining a worthless painting

A financial analyst in Philadelphia bought a painting for $4 in 1989. He bought it because he liked the frame. The canvas of the painting had a tear in it, so the man decided to remove the frame from the banal image. As he attempted to separate it from the art, the frame fell apart in his hands. This revealed a document between the canvas and its wood backing.

It looked like an old copy of the Declaration of Independence. At the prompting of a friend, he had the document appraised. It was an original copy of the famous pronouncement, printed in 1776. At the time, there were only 23 copies of this series, two of which were privately owned.

The document was sold at auction, fetching $2.42 million!

If this man had never looked more closely at his purchased artwork, he would have never discovered its actual value.

When we accept self-blame, we fail to look closer at ourselves. We are avoiding the discomfort of self-reflection at the cost of our own value. We see the things painted on the surface—our tendencies and habits—and mistake them for our unchangeable nature.

In truth, there is much we can change if we do not settle for the distraction of self-blame.

One more thought: How appropriate is it that the treasure found by the man in Philadelphia was the Declaration of Independence? When we dig deeper and separate ourselves from the attributes layered on top of us, we find an essential sense of independence. We see the freedom to transform and rediscover ourselves.

Imposters and bestselling authors

When researcher and author Amy Cuddy turned 19, she was injured in a devastating car wreck. She was thrown from the vehicle and sustained a severe head injury, resulting in major cognitive issues. Contrary to what the medical experts told her, Cuddy eventually graduated from college. Though it took her an extra four years.

She pursued a doctorate and followed her adviser Susan Fisk to Princeton University. During her first year, she didn't feel like she belonged; she was self-conscious about the effects of her head injury. On the eve of a presentation Cuddy feared would expose her as a fraud, she told her adviser she was quitting. Fisk wouldn't hear of it.

You're going to stay, and this is what you're going to do. You are going to fake it. You're going to do every talk that you ever get asked to do.

The Princeton adviser continued:

You're just going to do it and do it and do it, even if you're terrified and paralyzed and having an out-of-body experience, until you have this moment where you say, 'Oh my gosh, I'm doing it. Like, I have become this. I am actually doing this.'

Cut to the chase: Amy Cuddy proudly obtained her Doctorate in Philosophy, then taught at the Kellogg School of Management and Harvard Business School. The story above is from her TED Talk on the power of body language, which has been viewed over 64 million times. Her *New York Times* Bestseller *Presence* has sold over half a million copies and has been published in 35 languages.

To my mind, this does not sound like a fake.

She does not fit the description of an imposter.

Yet that is precisely what Cuddy felt like in the beginning.

If you feel like an imposter at certain moments in your life—congratulations! You're a member of the human race. Every person feels like an imposter sometimes. This is especially true when trying something different, like a learning a new language or new sport. At work, imposter thoughts fill our brain with a new job or promotion.

If you have bouts of imposter syndrome and something goes wrong with a project, it's no surprise when you blame yourself for the shortfall. You already feel inadequate and out of place. A failure affirms those suspicions.

If imposter syndrome is rare for you, be aware that others struggle with it and may be too quick to accept blame for mistakes and failures that are not theirs.

The dilemmas of Shawshank

In game theory, the prisoner's dilemma is a thought experiment in which two people are challenged with a unique problem: cooperate with one another for mutual reward or betray the other for one's individual benefit.

In our case, imagine that two criminals worked in concert to commit a single crime. The police arrest them and separate the accused into different rooms and offer them the same two deals.

Deal one: Remain silent and potentially serve no time. This means running the risk of doing the full term because one's partner pleads guilty in order to get a reduced sentence.

Deal two: Confess to the crime and 'rat out' one's partner. Then only serve half the sentence while their partner endures the whole punishment.

A lesser-known version of this scenario is called the innocent prisoner's dilemma. In the movie *Shawshank Redemption*, Andy—played by actor Tim Robbins—is convicted of murdering his wife and her lover in a crime of passion. Andy maintains his innocence throughout his trial and time in prison, but there's one scene where guilt overwhelms him. As he speaks to Morgan Freeman's character, Red, Andy opens up:

> *My wife used to say I'm a hard man to know. Like a closed book. Complained about it all the time. She was beautiful. I loved her. But I guess I couldn't show it enough.*

> *I killed her, Red.*

> *I didn't pull the trigger. But I drove her away. That's why she died. Because of me, the way I am.*

Even though he knows he didn't commit the crime, Andy feels he's the one to blame.

In an interesting contrast, we see Red sit before a parole board three times in the movie. The first two times, he says what he thinks the board wants to hear. That he is reformed and no longer a danger to society. Despite his stating this, his parole is rejected both times.

After serving 30 years of his life sentence, Red is up for his third attempt at parole. This time, he is a broken man who seems resigned to his imprisonment. The board asks if he is sorry for what he did.

> There's not a day goes by I don't feel regret. Not because I'm in here, or because you think I should. I look back on the way I was then: a young, stupid kid who committed that terrible crime.

Red's face seems to soften.

> I want to talk to him. I want to try and talk some sense to him, tell him the way things are. But I can't. That kid's long gone and this old man is all that's left.

The film highlights the problem of extolling your innocence in prison. At one point, Red says he's the only guilty man in Shawshank. Everyone else unjustifiably states they're innocent. These hollow claims mean that the pleas of any truly innocent man fall on deaf ears. Also, Red's parole hearings make it clear that admitting guilt is essential to be granted parole.

Andy never gets a hearing, but if he did, he would've faced the innocent prisoner's dilemma. Maintaining his innocence would have hurt his opportunity for parole.

Innocence and guilt

This is true in today's prisons as well. Parole boards do not have the resources to investigate whenever a prisoner claims they were unjustly convicted. For the sake of expedience, they are presumed guilty. A prisoner's refusal to accept guilt is seen as a lack of remorse.

Since the stated goal of prison is rehabilitation (which Red claims is a word made up so the parole board will have a job), accepting guilt and showing remorse are required for parole.

The dilemma for a genuinely innocent prisoner is that accepting guilt for something they didn't do eliminates any possibility of their exoneration. They may gain their freedom, but they will never be considered innocent.

In our workplaces, blame culture can operate as its own prison system and parole board.

When a person is presumably to blame for an issue at work, their claims of innocence often hurt them. Skeptical teammates and supervisors easily interpret such proclamations as dishonesty and view their lack of remorse as an attempt to escape rightly-deserved consequences. As a result, similarly to our justice system, an innocent person may experience harsher effects by claiming innocence instead of accepting guilt.

If you are unfairly blamed, recognize the forces are working against you. Know it may take more than a claim of innocence to avoid being accused.

On the other hand, if you are blaming another person, especially if you're a leader, be aware that when someone receives and accepts blame, it isn't always proof of their guilt. Some will unjustly take responsibility to avoid harsher consequences.

Flushing earthquakes

I would define suffering very simply as whenever you are not in control.

Father Richard Rohr

I once heard a story about a California mom potty training her son. He stood up, pulled up his pants, and was flushing the toilet just as an earthquake began. The room started to shake, and items fell off counters and shelves. His mom dropped down to hold and protect him, but mercifully the quake ended quickly.

As the mother stood back up, the little boy looked at her with wide eyes. He glanced down at the toilet, then back up at his mom and uttered sincerely:

"What did I do?"

We laugh about the boy's naïve question. Of course, he had not caused the earthquake. His toilet flushing correlated with the house shaking only because he was in that particular place at that specific time. Yet we ask this of ourselves about situations over which we had little or no influence. "What did I do?" Even though we may have simply been in a particular place at a specific time.

This tendency may come from a sense of guilt, but it could be something else entirely: our desire to be in control. When we have no power over what caused an issue in our lives, we admit we may be unable to solve it.

It's easy to see how blaming others can be a sign of having control issues. Self-blaming can be just as much about control, but it charades under another name—responsibility.

Shooting my chemical messengers

Let's return to my story of being admitted to the hospital after going numb at the carpet store. When we last discussed it, I was in bed, wracked with pain.

The doctors had run some tests, but nothing was conclusive. They were now waiting to see my status the following day. My wife Tammy went home to be with the kids while my dad stayed with me.

Slowly, I succumbed to the morphine, finally escaping the agony by falling asleep. But, in the middle of the night, I woke up. Without thinking much about it, I sat up, slipped out of bed, and strolled to the bathroom. A minute or two later as I returned to bed, my father awoke from his uncomfortable sleep on a hospital couch. He was startled and confused.

Just hours ago, I was completely debilitated. Now, like a miracle, I was walking around—Lazarus emerging from the tomb. And I seemed perfectly fine. I was talking with my father, yet struggled somewhat to think clearly. I no longer had a headache, but my mind felt a bit cloudy. Otherwise, I was normal again.

The next morning, an MRI showed there was no damage to my brain. Other tests were positive as well. A neurologist reviewed my records and asked me a few questions about my stress and health history. I shared how my economic circumstances had been at a boil lately. How stressed I was about taking care of my family.

Based on my test result, she ruled out a mini-stroke. Instead, the doctor diagnosed that I likely had a rare condition called a sporadic hemiplegic migraine. The condition is 'sporadic' because there was no history of this type of migraine in my family, so it likely wasn't hereditary. The term 'hemiplegic' refers to the paralysis of one side of my body.

Today I understand that this condition caused a breakdown in my body's ability to make a specific protein. Without that protein, my nerve cells had trouble sending out or taking in signals between each other.

One of these necessary chemical messengers is serotonin. This neurotransmitter is responsible for multiple functions. It can help regulate our mood, cognitive function, learning ability, memory, reward centers, and constriction of our blood vessels.

I believe the stress and resentment created in the wake of my business collapsing contributed heavily to this event, triggering a condition that was lurking dormant in my body. Part of my stress was the multifaceted blame I held against myself, my former partner, and the circumstances around my business failure.

Not only did I need to seek medical treatments for my condition, but I had to find a new way to deal with my stress and resentment. I had to get the venomous poison out of my system so it would no longer debilitate me.

Aftershocks

Nearly two years later, on the day before Valentine's Day, Tammy showed me a video of news coverage for the Grammy Awards ceremony. With the Staples Center in the background, local CBS affiliate reporter Serene Branson stood holding her microphone with her makeup and hair looking perfect. She breaks from her cheerful smile to deliver the story leading up to the music awards show.

But what comes out of her mouth is total gibberish. Her facial expression changes to fear and confusion. I immediately know what is happening. My throat tightens, and tears well up in my eyes and stream down my cheeks. Many concluded she was drunk; others assumed she had a stroke. Like me, Serene had a severe migraine.

Even as I rewatched the YouTube video of her report recently to write this book, it struck a nerve. It's the same when I see portrayals of aneurisms in movies or TV shows. There are times I find myself sobbing uncontrollably. I try and assure myself that I'm okay. I didn't actually have a stroke; it wasn't that serious. But my emotions don't listen to my logic. The tears continue to come.

Seeing something so similar to my experience reminds me of the helplessness I felt that day more than twelve years ago. The intense fear I had when I realized my life could end at any moment. The surreal experience of family, friends, and clergy comforting Tammy in front of me while I could not respond under my heavy medications.

Everyone believed my life was hanging in the balance.

It's a reminder that sneaks up and surprises me when I least expect it, slapping me in the face with a message I cannot ignore. Do not take life for granted.

Life is too short for resentment. The real tragedy would be to let bitterness steal what little time we have left.

PART 4

Beyond Blame

10

"*Reprimanding 'bad apples' is like peeing in your pants.
You did something about the problem and feel relieved.
But then it gets cold and uncomfortable. And you look like a fool.*"

Sydney Dekker, *The Field Guide to Understanding Human Error*

Beyond Blaming Others

Habits vs. culture

Culture is a grossly overused business buzzword nowadays, and it's used in many different ways. At the beginning of this book, I talked about culture being like the water we swim in. Because we're always in it, we aren't aware it exists, let alone how much it influences us.

A little later, I shared this definition of culture:

Individual behavior over time = habit.
Group behaviors over time = culture.

This maxim helps us to be aware of culture's existence, giving us a method by which to influence it. As Winston Churchill said, "We shape our buildings. After that, they shape us." Recognizing culture as our group behavior over time opens an opportunity to shape the culture we are a part of, which then will shape us.

But what is the starting point? For many of us, we're shaping a corporate culture where expediency may trump effectiveness. For example, we handle important decisions over text messages or email threads instead of with face-to-face discussions.

What's the alternative? How about we establish clear criteria for decision-making, knowing who needs to be involved, what data is needed, and how to process it? By doing this, we are architecting a culture of clarity and purpose.

How you deal with blame over time is your blame habit. How your team deals with blame over time becomes your blame culture. And that overall tone—the background buzz of blame—will shape you and your team members into the future.

When we understand this truth, we realize that we cannot afford to ignore culture—even if we feel it's been discussed ad nauseam. What if the opposite were true? Maybe it's possible that we haven't engaged enough about it or discussed the topic with sufficient depth.

Leading: Bringing others with you

If blaming essentially means giving away your power and thus saying "no" to yourself, taking responsibility means reclaiming your power and thus saying "yes" to yourself.

By giving up the blame game and assuming responsibility for your relationships and your needs, you can go right to the root of the conflict and take the lead in transforming... your life.

William Ury, *Getting To Yes With Yourself*

Another way to define leadership is bringing others on a journey. Whether or not you have been given authority, you can still lead. Author Seth Godin calls this type of leadership being a "linchpin" (and I highly recommend his book of the same name). You need to influence others to persuade others to join you.

At the start, your influence may be a byproduct of reputation or charisma, but having a worthy destination also contributes to your ability to lead. Once you've identified what's wrong with the current culture, share a compelling vision of what the future could be. There's a good chance others will follow you there.

When you change your habits to avoid blame, you are leading by example. Others will notice you responding differently to failures. When, instead of reflexively seeking a scapegoat after a mistake, you ask insightful questions—you alter the paradigm. It's like a breath of fresh air. Still, leading by example is not enough.

You need to invite your teammates to join you. But how?

Talk about blame

Part of why blame is acceptable is because it hides in the darkness. When we bring it out into the light, it loses its potency. As I shared earlier, the Scapegoat Mechanism only works when society believes the scapegoat is blameworthy. Likewise, when we realize blame is being used unfairly, we are less likely to enable a culture of blame.

Clarify and differentiate

Communicate explicitly that there is a difference between blame, responsibility, and accountability. Blame is a sense of resentment toward those we hold at fault for misfortune. Responsibility is taking immediate ownership of one's actions. Accountability is letting others hold us responsible for current and future actions.

Share the vision

Talk with others about the benefits of blameless culture. Explain how you can better exemplify responsibility and accountability without scapegoating and experiencing the toxic effects of blame. Most people will agree with this concept, but may wonder if it's possible. Help them realize blameless culture is achievable when you work together and reinforce your group behavior over time.

Blame this book

Recommend this book to coworkers. Loan your copy to others. If you're a leader, consider providing copies to those on your team. Hold a book study or give a short presentation on the principles. It doesn't matter how you share this message, the most important thing is you help it to spread. Feel free to take a photo of a page that impacted you and share it with your team.

Share the tools

In Chapter 12, you'll find a list of tools you can apply to yourself and with your team. These can be used by leaders or by a small team. For large organizations, it may be helpful to apply changes to your overall practices to increase the opportunity for success.

Leaving: Time to move on?

If you feel your workplace is toxic, how long do you stay if things don't change? This can be a challenging question to answer.

First, if you don't feel physically safe in your work environment, you should leave if leadership won't address the issues immediately. Even if you work in an industry with assumed risks, like emergency response or washing windows on skyscrapers, you should be assured that your employer has taken or will take steps to mitigate those risks reasonably and quickly.

If you don't feel psychologically safe in your workplace, you need to answer a few questions to determine if and when it's time to leave. For example, who is creating the toxicity?

If it's an individual, Dr. Travis Bradbury, co-author of *Emotional Intelligence 2.0*, gives a few tips for handling toxic people.

1. Set limits on how much time you spend with toxic people.

2. Realize that difficult people are often irrational, so trying to beat them at their own game is a waste of time. Don't react to their emotional baggage. Respond proactively to the facts.

3. Be aware of your own emotions. This may require you to take time out and evaluate your feelings.

4. Establish boundaries that make it clear you are responsible for your feelings, attitudes, and behaviors. You're not responsible for those of other people, especially difficult people.

5. Choose your battles wisely and stand your ground only when the time is right.

6. Don't focus on the problem. Focus on solutions. Spend less time worrying about the toxic person and more attention on how you will deal with them.

7. Forgive, but don't forget. Show grace, but don't let the same issues continue to occur.

8. Don't give into negative self-talk. It will send you on a downward spiral and serves no practical purpose.

9. Practice self-care. Be sure to get the sleep you need. Take appropriate breaks. Enjoy your time with family and friends. Don't let toxic coworkers ruin your life at work and at home.

10. Use your support system—someone in your life, at work or outside, is in your corner. Spend time with them and seek out their insights regarding your issue. Realize it's okay to ask for help. You don't have to do this alone.

If leadership creates toxicity, changing the culture will likely take more time. So, consider some additional questions:

1. How patient can you be with change?

If you feel your mental health is suffering too much to wait for change, consider a shorter timeline for leaving. Take some time off to regain perspective along with your mental health. This can help you assess how long you can wait for noticeable change to occur.

But set your timeline ahead of time. Whether you need a month, three months, or a year, you should decide up front. Otherwise, you may continue to make excuses for waiting and never pull the trigger. Setting a timeline first also allows you to research jobs and network for your next possible opportunity. You may find a healthier work environment with better opportunities

2. Are you seeing signs that anything will change?

This needs to be more than lip service. Are actions being taken? Is leadership willing to put in a reasonable effort, time, and possibly a financial commitment to make change happen? Or are you hearing excuses and dismissive responses when issues are brought to light?

3. Are you speaking the same language?

Maybe leadership is willing to commit to a healthier work culture, but they don't have the language and tools to cope with it. Share some insights from this book to help clarify that responsibility and accountability are possible without using blame.

Verify whether leadership values psychological safety at work. If their values are not in line with yours, then there is a good chance this is a cultural misalignment. But this is difficult to evaluate if there is no agreement on the definition and significance of these terms.

Choosing when to move on is a subjective decision. Ultimately, you want to be sure you're realistic with your situation. Avoid making knee-jerk decisions and assess what you can accept and what is likely to change.

Ice to Eskimos

I spent a chunk of my career in business management consulting. I was in a boutique consulting firm that had made a name for itself by transforming traditional, more industrial businesses (think Big Oil) into learning organizations. While most technology companies and mainstream businesses had already made this transformation, many major oil and gas companies had not.

This was good business for the better part of a decade.

When I joined the company, even the laggard oil companies had adopted this model. Eventually, I realized the company was hanging onto a formula that had been a very lucrative cash cow, but now they had milked that cow dry. Prospective new customers would hear our pitch and respond, "We already do that."

To use another analogy, we were trying to sell ice to Eskimos.

Instead of doing actual market research and identifying new opportunities to help transform the industry, leadership encouraged our staff to ask stakeholders questions like, "What is keeping you up at night?" Then respond by letting them know we could help with those issues—regardless of what they may be.

While this strategy wasn't terrible in the short term, there was no concerted effort to look at common threads across different departments and companies. There was little development work performed to create new products and services.

Consultants became short-order cooks who took orders from clients and then reheated leftover proposals and projects.

Leadership never acknowledged the core business model had grown stale. They ignored the trouble until it found them in the form of an oil crash. In 2015, the price of oil fell to less than $50 per barrel.

This was below the cost most companies spent producing the oil. In other words, they were losing money on each barrel they sold.

The industry cut costs dramatically. Staff was laid off. All non-critical projects were halted. New projects were denied. The firm I worked for went through round after round of staff cuts. I saw friends losing their jobs every week.

I was fortunate to work on a project my client hadn't canceled, but I knew my contract would not be renewed once that project was complete. By the time I left the company, 80% of its consultants had left or were laid off.

The firm never recovered from that market crash.

I say this because you may be a leader in an organization and the previous discussion of job hunting made you nervous. If so, consider this. The more your employees accept toxic behavior, the less impetus you have to make a change. Maybe being a little nervous is a good thing. Use that concern to fuel action. You can't just ignore potentially toxic work issues and expect them to disappear.

Leading by looking for trouble

Mark Modesti, a close friend of mine, gave a fantastic TED Talk entitled "The Argument for Trouble." He cited a statistic that 40% of Fortune 500 companies won't be around in ten years.

He proposed this was because they avoided trouble instead of looking for it. Similar to Blockbuster, who had the opportunity to buy Netflix twice. These current top companies will make unwise decisions because they ignore crises until it's too late.

In his talk, Mark brought up Abraham Lincoln as an example of someone who looked for trouble. In the 1850s, Lincoln had a track record of losing—in business and politics. But he eventually won the most critical election when he became President.

Instead of resting on that win and making his time in office as easy as possible, Lincoln surrounded himself with his opponents—appointing many of them to his administration. This famed leader, who ended up guiding the US through the tumult of the Civil War, knew his advisors/adversaries would fight against him on critical issues. He also knew they were strong individuals who would give him insight into the opposing party's views.

Mark wrapped up his TED Talk by mentioning two kinds of trouble. First, there's the kind we should avoid and run from. Then there's another kind that wants to take us somewhere—a trouble that can grow us and stretch us. The kind of trouble we should run toward. The kind of trouble that's worth the trouble. I wonder if this is what Civil Rights leader John Lewis called "good trouble."

If you have issues with a blame culture or a generally toxic workplace atmosphere, it won't help to ignore the risk that your employees will leave if things don't change. Actively look for this kind of trouble so that you can address it.

This allows you to improve your workplace and have a shot at retaining your best employees. Don't make all that effort to recruit and onboard your talented workforce—to just watch them walk out the door because you ignored a dysfunctional culture.

Additionally, if your employees see you are addressing blame and toxicity in the workplace, they'll be more likely to bring awareness to issues you haven't recognized. Like Lincoln's 'team of rivals,' they will be more willing to contribute to the solution because they know you're committed to fixing it.

Addressing blame culture and a toxic work atmosphere can be a lot of trouble. But I'd argue—and my friend Mark would agree—it's the kind of trouble that's worth the risk.

The anti-scapegoat

The week after the death of Queen Elizabeth II in September 2022, neuroscientist and author Sam Harris shared an observation about the purpose of royalty on his podcast *Making Sense*.

> *A monarch, when she or he is actually functioning as intended, is the opposite of a scapegoat.*

He went on to suggest that Elizabeth II performed the function of anti-scapegoat exceptionally well. She was the embodiment—not of British society's sins—but of their virtues. Even uncommon virtues they didn't have like discipline, dignity, self-restraint, and self-sacrifice. She represented the stability, civility, and patriotism the country needed to persevere through many crises.

A tribute article from British-American writer Andrew Sullivan inspired Harris. Sullivan described the dramatic implications of this young woman ascending to the throne to become Queen of England.

Elizabeth Windsor was tasked as a twenty-something with a job that required her to say or do nothing that could be misconstrued, controversial, or even interestingly human—for the rest of her life.

Sullivan went on to emphasize her impact on British culture:

> As long as she was there, [these virtues] were at the center of an idea of Britishness that helped define the culture at its best.

The Queen was not a celebrity or an idol. She was not a vestige of conventional popularity. Meanwhile, due in large part to her integrity in her private and public life, she was also not someone who could easily be mocked. She did not pick political sides, as she represented all Britons. She was willing to be a symbol.

Not through her death but through her life.

Not unwillingly, but voluntarily.

She was an anti-scapegoat. Something great leaders aspire to be. One who lifts people out of their divisiveness and hopelessness. An embodiment of the group's virtues. A representation of all their employees, not just a select few.

This is a much more powerful choice—and infinitely more challenging—than dividing people against each other through blame and fear.

New habits for individuals

If habits are for individuals and culture is for the group, then leadership is at the intersection of habits and culture. The patterns of leaders impact the culture of the group and vice-versa.

Thus, for anyone to break the blame habit requires an act of self-leadership. It involves understanding what triggers cause you to react and fall into this bad habit, and choosing an alternative instead.

Charles Duhigg, the author of *The Power of Habit*, explains habits by breaking them down into three essential elements: a cue, a routine, and a reward.

Whatever triggers your habit is the cue. This could be a meeting with a supervisor when you know you haven't accomplished your goals. You anticipate being chided. The resulting insecurity causes you to search for excuses.

These cues send you into your routine. A blame habit routine may be blaming yourself or others. If you blame yourself, your sense of value is shaped by your insecurities. You may believe you're to blame because of a flaw in your character, "I'm too lazy"—because of incompetence, "I'm not good enough or smart enough"—or because of your fate, "I'm cursed, I must have the worst luck."

The other blame routine involves others. You may lay the blame on a coworker, "He didn't contribute his fair share to the project"— or the company, "They didn't give us enough time or budget to do the job right"—or even something as remote as the nation's current leader, "Their economic policy made the market unstable."

Now, what about the reward? In Duhigg's model, he talks about rewards like cookies, juicy gossip, or a beautiful walk alongside a lake. What is the reward for blame?

It can vary, but primarily it's the release of the tension created by a failure. It's the lightning strike that releases the electrical charge in the atmosphere. We're just deciding where to put the lightning rod. Other rewards could be retaining our status or reputation, inflicting misfortune on someone who previously hurt you, or just putting someone else in their place.

By recognizing blame as a habit, we can know how we use and abuse it. We can see the components of it (cue, routine, reward). And we can choose to adjust our habits by selecting a new routine or reward when we recognize a cue is triggering our typical response.

Interrupting automaticity

> *The unexamined life is not worth living.*
>
> Socrates

We fail to examine life when we resort to blaming instead of studying for solutions. People are often scapegoated simply because their accusers were on auto-pilot. We blame others out of habit or because it is the cultural water we have been swimming in. Either way, we may not even realize we are doing it.

Psychologists call this effect of acting out of habit without thinking 'automaticity.' This helpful skill allows us to accomplish routine tasks without concentrating on them. Walking, riding a bike, speaking, reading, and even driving a car are often automatized tasks. It benefits us by not burning energy but allows us to do other tasks simultaneously. Unfortunately, this is a reason why so many drivers are guilty of flirting with dangerous distractions like texting while driving.

That brings up the negative aspect of automaticity. It allows us to make harmful choices without contemplating what we are doing, why we are doing it, and the potential consequences of those choices. This is why we plan to sleep early and crawl into our bed, only to find ourselves doom-scrolling on social media hours later.

It takes intentionality to side-step these habits and consider other possibilities. We must engage our brain's executive functions to snap out of our habits and automatic thinking. If we have a habit of blaming others, we need reminders to snap us out of auto-pilot.

Here are a few tips for interrupting automaticity:

Set an alert

Set an alert on your phone. You can start by setting it to alert you every hour during the day. After a few days, you may notice you're aware before the reminders alert you. Then, you can change it to every three or four hours. After a week or so, you can have it remind you once in the morning and once at night.

STOP

Another option is to use the acronym STOP (Sit, Think, Organize, Perform). Schedule 15 minutes each day to sit still, think about what you're doing and what is essential, organize what you will do going forward, then perform what you just planned. Some recommend doing this daily, weekly, and monthly. More time is needed to think through and organize your week or month so you can block off 30 minutes and one hour, respectively.

Write a Post-It note

A straightforward option is to have a reminder in front of you. You can keep this book near your keyboard so you see it often. You could put a sticky note on your monitor. The risk of this method is you may start to ignore the reminder after you are used to seeing it.

Living a balanced life

Take care of yourself by doing things you probably already know you should be doing. This includes getting sufficient sleep, eating healthy foods, and getting at least 20 minutes of exercise each day. When your body is rested, fueled, and engaged, it is easier to stay alert.

Break up your routine

Take an occasional walk to get away from your desk and engage with a new environment. Change your position from sitting to standing, even just for a few minutes (a sit/stand desk is excellent for this).

A new culture for groups

People like us do things like this.

Seth Godin

Changing a work culture is different than changing a habit. We have all seen how challenging it can be to kick a bad personal habit like a poor diet, smoking, or gambling.

Changing a work culture can be even more daunting.

You're dealing with dozens, hundreds, or even thousands of people. How do you change the way they all use, manage, and react to blame? It can seem impossible.

What does it look like for every aspect of your team, company, or organization to function without blame?

Strategy

Your goals and how you will achieve them should be geared toward results. Your strategy should also load balance responsibility across different departments. If the strategy for the company's success is overwhelmingly reliant on sales, you are setting up a scenario where sales may be blamed for a failure they could not avoid. Identify how other departments will support success and share responsibility.

Management

Leadership's response to failure should focus on solving the problem, not associating blame. Moreover, leaders must show transparency with their mistakes. By hiding their own failures, leaders imply two things. First, they indicate they believe they are infallible. This is simply inauthentic. The other implication is that there is no grace for failures. Otherwise, why would they be hiding it?

Communication

There should be clarity around roles, responsibilities, and how people will be accountable for their results. The culture should be one where individuals can openly discuss blame, call it out, and encourage each other to avoid abusing it.

Employee Experience

Employees should not be held to a double standard because they are different from others in the group. Individuals who are seen as outsiders are more often the target of scapegoating. Be sure your culture is inclusive instead of creating 'us' and 'them' mentalities.

Structure

How teams are organized and collaborate should foster teamwork instead of creating rivalries. Teams should be able to support each other's goals, but be sure that overlap doesn't create opportunities for finger-pointing. Although there are shared goals, the responsibilities of each group should be distinct. Dependencies should be clarified, so it is understood when one group's failure impacts others.

Systems

It is critical that data is managed and tracked effectively by your tools. If there is a failure or mistake, then this data can be the forensic evidence providing the necessary clues to understand what went wrong and how it can be fixed. A healthy culture understands the importance of the tools and data in supporting success.

By addressing the above organizational dynamics, a healthier workplace culture can begin to take shape. Individuals can feel supported, and leaders can feel equipped to guide their teams.

A bias for action

We have a 'strategic plan.' It's called doing things.

Herb Kelleher, co-founder of Southwest Airlines

It's hard to spend much time blaming others when your organization is busy getting things done. While writing their seminal business book *In Search of Excellence,* business consultants Tom Peters and Bob Waterman coined the term "bias for action" to describe one of the defining attributes of excellent companies. Peters even claimed this was the most important attribute of business success.

In an action-biased culture, blame is a waste of time and energy. It impedes moving forward. Blame also opposes many of the characteristics of a company that prioritizes action.

These organizations emphasize their people's ability to make decisions and execute. Blame helps neither of these priorities. Decisions are clouded, and execution can be delayed or burdened by a fear of blame.

Bold decisions to make progress may be sidelined for seemingly safer decisions that, conversely, possess less upside. Opportunities to improve execution may be disregarded in favor of doing it the way it's always been done and avoiding criticism for straying from the status quo.

Action requires planning for impact and progress. Blame can oppose these goals. Instead of making an impact, individuals try to avoid the spotlight. Flying under the radar becomes more critical than achieving progress. It becomes more acceptable to lower goals to something unremarkable instead of putting your neck on the line for something that will genuinely move the needle.

When you have a bias for action, you're willing to try new things you aren't sure will succeed. Fear of blame opposes that by forcing people to look for guarantees—doing the things that have already been done, things that are proven to work. This imposes the status quo on teams and individuals. It stifles growth and innovation as new ideas are discarded in favor of the 'tried and true.'

A focus on action means you plan ahead. You anticipate the obstacles that might get in the way of your goals. It requires candid conversations about the reality of your situation. Blame cultures discourage this kind of communication. Admitting something may be complex or problematic may get you labeled as a nay-sayer. By avoiding frank discussions about potential issues, you also avoid considering possible solutions that could accelerate your progress and help you achieve more in the long run.

Action cultures are learning cultures. They learn by doing. They learn by failing. They learn through discussions and feedback. Blame can hinder all of these activities. It creates a cloud of fear that inhibits learning. Blame stops learning in its tracks because finger-pointing seems like a solution itself.

After a failure, someone is blamed. They are punished, and the group moves on. We believe we learned what the problem was by identifying a scapegoat. Instead, we accept the pseudo-solution of blame while ignoring systemic issues like ineffective processes, inaccurate information, and insufficient resources.

We miss out on opportunities to identify core issues, address them, and improve our ability to achieve future success. The result is often repeating the same mistakes in perpetuity.

Action-bias helps companies:
- Prioritize decision-making and execution
- Plan for impact and progress
- Try new things
- Anticipate road blocks and obstacles
- Organize for learning

Embracing a bias for action is an effective way to deemphasize blame in your work culture. You appreciate effective planning, innovation, and learning, and results. Blame is seen as the hindrance it truly is, as well as a tool for advancing self-interests and avoiding criticism or punishment.

Accountability and heroic effort

Moving beyond blame doesn't mean you toss accountability out the window. On the contrary, by moving beyond blame, you can identify the root cause of your issues and address them. This includes any irresponsible or destructive actions.

After a failure, those who contributed to mistakes are often scapegoated, while those who performed heroic efforts to try and salvage the situation are simultaneously praised. This seems logical.

I mean, what's wrong with heroic effort?

There's nothing inherently wrong with it. But heroic effort is typically a sign of systemic issues. If organizations overemphasize valiant effort while ignoring the root causes in the system, then the problems will not be resolved, and a hero will be needed again.

As Mr. Incredible says in Pixar's animated film *The Incredibles*:

> *No matter how many times you save the world, it always manages to get back in jeopardy again. Sometimes I just want it to stay saved! You know, for a little bit? I feel like the maid; I just cleaned up this mess! Can we keep it clean for... for ten minutes!*

Like Mr. Incredible, top performers can get tired of "saving the world" repeatedly when leadership never addresses the cause of the problem.

When organizations focus on the root cause of failures, they still may identify individual contributions to the loss and hold those persons accountable. Moreover, flaws in the system and processes will also be identified. These can be addressed, so it is less likely the same issues will recur.

Unless there is a need for regulatory or criminal investigation, most organizations penalize individuals and go no further. Even if they fire the offending contributors—or the innocent, in the case of scapegoating—it may do very little to deter another similar incident in the future.

An Uber-sized mistake

Cease to blame employees for problems of the system. Management should be held responsible for faults of the system.

W. Edwards Deming, *Out of the Crisis*

Jeff Lawson is the CEO of Twilio, a company that creates tools for developers. Back in 2017, Uber—one of Twilio's largest clients—announced it would cut its spending with the firm. This had to be disclosed to investors, which significantly impacted the company.

"Our stock took a huge hit. I think it fell 40% in one day," Lawson said. He also admitted he was tempted to blame the employee responsible for Uber's account. Instead of using them as a scapegoat, he decided to pay attention to why Uber scaled back.

"We found out that the real problem was—we had under-staffed sales," says Mr Lawson. "The Uber account had been growing very quickly, but the salesperson did not have enough time to take care of the client properly."

"If we had had a bigger sales team," he added, "they would have spoken to Uber much more often and would have picked up on their problems with our service. They were just one account of about thirty that this salesperson had. Uber should have had a dedicated account manager."

This information made it apparent that the solution wasn't to fire anyone. On the contrary, they decided to hire more.

Lawson increased the sales staff so they would have the capacity to manage their accounts more effectively. When your biggest client cuts back, it could signal a decline. Instead, Twilio grew five-fold. Lawson attributes much credit to their new process for addressing mistakes and setbacks, called 'blameless post-mortems.'

"Every employee will make mistakes. That's unavoidable," Lawson said. "As leaders, we have to build systems in which mistakes are non-catastrophic. If you have created a system where one person can ruin the entire company, then you as a leader are at fault."

Blame for variation

In any work task, there will be variations in performance. Renowned quality and systems guru W. Edwards Deming estimated that 94% of the variation in worker performance is based on the systems and processes, not the workers themselves.

When nearly all subpar performance can be attributed to these two factors, why do we respond to mistakes and failures by blaming individuals? Deming says it's because we believe these variations are a sign there was a particular cause. Something out of the ordinary must be at fault for the issue. But, as it turns out, the fault can almost always be found in the ordinary.

The system causes most issues. Instead of analyzing systemic problems, our biased thinking drives us to mistakenly focus on blaming an individual. Then, after we scapegoat that person by firing them or demoting them, someone else will be the unlucky victim of a systemic issue that was never addressed.

Blame hinders our ability to solve interesting problems.

Crazy Shirts

My friend Fredrick Haugen told me the story of how he interviewed with a clothing manufacturer and retailer called Crazy Shirts. This iconic Hawaiian company designs, prints, and sells original t-shirts evocative of their flamboyant island personality.

It was apparent they had a unique approach to company culture. Their office building sits in the middle of a tropical garden and was built with a beautiful yellow cedar exterior. The open-concept interior is laden with antiques, including model airplanes and a full-sized statue of an ukulele musician. Coworkers affectionately called each other 'Crazies.' The break room, filled with free fruits and juices, overlooks an oasis of plant life and spectacular scenery.

But what the HR director told Fredrick in her office before the tour spoke volumes about the commitment Crazy Shirts made to their employees. She explained that they kept detailed records on the output of each individual retail employee. They knew the top and bottom performers for every store.

Then she asked, "What do you think we do with the bottom ten percent of our salespeople?"

Fredrick shrugged, "Put them on notice? Fire them?"

The director shook her head, "Not at all. We match them up with a top performer, even if they're at another store. They learn to do the job well from another 'Crazy' like them."

As Fredrick shared this story with me, I was impressed with the dedication of the company's leaders. They saw a new hire as a long-term commitment to partner with. They were committed to mutual success. This attitude came right from the top, Crazy Shirts founder Rick Ralston (who started the company on a Waikiki sidewalk in the '60s airbrushing art on t-shirts for tourists).

Honestly, I was even more surprised when he told me the interview occurred back in the mid-80s. Most companies today still hesitate to set aside blame and give employees the grace to learn from each other and grow from their mistakes.

IBM's 'Education Fund'

There is a story passed down over the years at IBM. In the 1930s, IBM was not the technology giant they are today. They were known for manufacturing tabulation machines and had created a new category called 'data processing.' Unfortunately, during the Great Depression, most companies were reducing their need for data as they laid off workers and had fewer time cards to calculate.

IBM CEO Thomas Watson was optimistic that demand would return after World War II, so he continued building and storing the machines instead of laying off his workers. Soon after the war, the company was desperate for increased sales.

According to the story, IBM lost a large government bid worth one million dollars. The salesman in charge of the opportunity appeared at Watson's office and laid an envelope on the CEO's desk. Watson knew it held a resignation letter. The salesman apologized for failing to win the bid.

"What happened?" asked Watson.

The salesman explained the details, sharing mistakes that were made and admitting what could have been done differently to win the bid. He thanked Watson for the opportunity to present and walked toward the door.

The mercurial CEO stopped the salesperson and handed the envelope back to him. He looked the dejected salesman in the eye and asked, "Why would I accept this when I have just invested one million dollars in your education?"

IBM later won enormous contracts with the U.S. Government due to the increased need for data processing in the wake of Franklin Delano Roosevelt's New Deal.

Watson's vision for the future of IBM drove him to hold out hope for his products and his people. His visionary brilliance may be one reason why the company eventually named its artificial intelligence supercomputer 'Watson.'

11

"You, yourself, as much as anyone else in the entire universe, deserve your love and affection."

Buddha

Beyond Blaming Ourselves

The Motivation Gap

One of the issues with blame culture is that it reduces employees' sense of autonomy and authority. We've all heard someone say they didn't seek permission first. Instead they ask for forgiveness later.

You're less likely to listen to that in a workplace where blame is prevalent because most individuals know they're more likely to get blame instead of forgiveness.

This contributes to the Motivation Gap.

Good leaders want employees to engage and contribute value to the organization. They do not want their teams to be frozen by a fear that blame will be assigned to them if their idea or project fails.

Yet, surveys convey a disturbingly high percentage of employees are not engaged in their work. Most research shows a 2:1 ratio. Roughly twice as many employees are not involved compared to those who are engaged.

At the same time, employees want a fulfilling work life and career. The research from the employee's perspective is not much better than from the leader's. Only half of workers were confident their job made a difference. What's even starker is that roughly 40% of overall respondents were convinced it would make no difference if their job disappeared.

Leaders want engagement. Employees want fulfillment.

Yet, the deficit between these intertwined needs has remained essentially unchanged for years. How can we bridge the engagement/fulfillment gap that leaders and employees want to fill?

Driven by AMPs

In his book *Drive*, Dan Pink identifies three areas that motivate us at work: autonomy, mastery, and purpose. One way to remember these elements is by using the acronym AMP.

Autonomy is the desire to direct our own lives. But it isn't the same as independence. Employees can't behave as if they have no accountability to their team or organization. Instead, they must acknowledge interdependence. They have a particular responsibility to the company and, in return, the company has obligations to them. Employees are responsible for being diligent in performing their duties. They are expected to take action and make difficult choices. And to do so within the company's value structure.

Mastery is the urge to get better at something that matters. This is a desire to reach our potential and pursue it continuously. Mastery is something we want for its own sake. Rewards and milestones are less important than the realization that we are improving.

Finally, purpose is the yearning to do our work in the service of something larger than ourselves. This often yields the highest levels of motivational potential. Being part of a cause, instead of simply a job, helps people apply themselves to their work without grumbling. It can also motivate them to solve incredibly complex problems as they associate a greater meaning to their work. It can cause the employee to care more about their results since it is related to a sense of great purpose.

What happens to the three aspects of AMP in a blame culture?

First off, it's hard for employees to enjoy a sense of autonomy. The lack of trust and employee empowerment undermines their sense of choice and control over their work. It's often unintentional, but blame-infused leaders tend to micromanage.

No matter how much leadership tries to cajole their employees into making decisions or contributing new ideas, it won't happen if workers know they'll be blamed every time something goes wrong. Without innovation and creativity, mastery is not possible.

Ultimately, a workplace steeped in blame saps any sense of purpose. Employees won't be empowered to bring their full potential without a sense of choice and control. Why would they put extra effort into their work—developing a sense of mastery—if they sense their company doesn't trust them? What's the point of trying?

Eat, Pray, Follow the Yellow Brick Road

Elizabeth Gilbert is the author of the bestselling memoir *Eat, Pray, Love*. In the wake of her novel's incredible success and its adaptation into a successful movie starring Julia Roberts, she gave a TED Talk on the pressures associated with creativity. She wrote a book on overcoming fear to live creatively.

Gilbert encourages everyone to embrace the fact that they are creative. She says the term 'creative person' is laughably redundant since creativity is a hallmark of being human. Our collective history is littered with examples of our innate creativity.

She warns us—in a similar fashion as our late, wizardly friend Gordon MacKenzie—that society will try to talk us out of our gift. Gilbert retorts, "they are wrong, and they are also annoying."

She reminds us that our creativity still resides within us. That inspiration is trying to find us, much as it did with our ancestors.

> *You do not need permission from the principal's office to live a creative life. Or if you worry that you need a permission slip, I just gave it to you. I just wrote it on the back of an old shopping list. Consider yourself fully accredited. Now make something.*

Gilbert passes permission slips out like candy at a parade. It's a form of autonomy that Dan Pink identified as an essential ingredient for motivation. If we look around, we see the concept of permission slips appear in many other places—some of them quite familiar.

Near the end of the classic film *The Wizard of Oz*, the young heroine Dorothy wants to return home to Kansas. She implores the Good Witch Glinda to help her on this quest.

Glinda smiles and says, "You don't need to be helped any longer. You've always had the power to go back to Kansas."

Dorothy is shocked, "I have?"

The Scarecrow then asks the frustrating question we all feel in these moments, "Then why didn't you tell her before?"

Glinda responds, "Because she wouldn't have believed me. She had to learn it for herself."

Dorothy suddenly realizes her AMP. That, during her journey to the Emerald City, she has attained autonomy, mastery, and purpose.

Just moments before, the Wizard of Oz had given Dorothy's friends (the Scarecrow, the Tin Man, and the Cowardly Lion) what they thought they lacked: a brain, a heart, and courage. But the tokens they received were merely placebos—a ceremonial form of permission slips. The trio had these characteristics all along. They were waiting for permission to believe in themselves.

We can spend our entire career, or life, seeking permission from others when we had the power all along. We ask the Munchkins, the Scarecrow, the Tin Man, the Cowardly Lion, and even the Wizard himself—only to discover we didn't need a permission slip. We had the ruby slippers on our feet from arrival.

You can write your own permission slip. Permission to do work that matters, to be a creative force, to take the next leap.

You have the power. You've always had the power. You may not believe me, but I hope you're willing to learn for yourself.

There is no anointing

Maybe you're procrastinating on doing something right now and blaming someone or something else to excuse your delay.

You don't feel ready. You're blaming it on a lack of preparation. You don't think you have enough money. You think you're not unique enough. You're blaming lousy luck.

Maybe you have this fantasy: Someone in a royal uniform will walk into the room in a tizzy. When he glances up and sees you, he sighs in relief and smiles.

"Oh, there you are! I've been looking all over for you!"

The royal servant walks over and sets down a very ornate box. He unclasps it and pulls the top half of the container away, revealing a beautiful crown resting on a pillow. Unseen trumpets blare in triumphant fanfare. A shaft of light shoots through a tall window and lands directly over you, illuminating your entire body.

The royal servant lifts the crown off the pillow as you kneel and lower your head. He gently but confidently places the crown on your head and declares in a loud voice for all to hear.

"By royal decree! I hereby announce Geraldine Musgrave can now start a podcast!"

This won't happen.

There is no anointing. There is no blessing you need to wait to graciously receive. The only permission you need is from yourself.

What are you waiting for?

Serenity Now

In an episode of *Seinfeld*, the character Frank—the father of Jerry's friend George Costanza—starts using the phrase "serenity now" as a relaxation technique whenever he feels angry. The irony is that Frank eventually finds himself yelling the phrase with explosive anger. The technique is actually making his anger worse.

Another character, Lloyd Braun, observes that Frank's attempt at "serenity now" instead is an unintentional way to repress his rage. In Braun's opinion, this only leads to "serenity now, insanity later."

Cue the show's funky solo bass riff here.

Of course, this playful dance on the theme of serenity has a strong precedence in modern culture—the Serenity Prayer, a staple saying of 12-step programs like Alcoholics Anonymous:

Father, give us courage to change what must be altered, Serenity to accept what cannot be helped, and the insight to know the one from the other.

This version was written by Winnifred Crane Wygal in a diary entry in 1932. As Wygal was a pupil of theologian Reinhold Niebuhr, it's now thought that he heard this aphorism in a sermon by Niebuhr.

This succinct and insightful mantra can help us all recognize where we have agency in life while not becoming overwhelmed or fretting over the things we cannot control or influence.

The prayer requests assistance with three aspects of a person's character: courage, serenity, and insight. Let's delve deeper into each of these petitions to understand the wisdom on offer.

"Courage to change what must be altered..."

Failures have consequences, some of which are unavoidable. In these moments, we must sidestep blame and instead have the courage to make necessary changes.

If a failure results in a significant financial shortfall, then it's logical that budgets must adjust to the new reality. In fact, spending cuts may need to occur. Yes, one can also look for changes that can increase your top line to offset lost revenue. But difficult decisions that require courage will need to be made. Try that first instead of seeking a scapegoat to take the heat.

"Serenity to accept what cannot be helped..."

Sometimes—no matter how much we want to change the outcome—it's simply out of our hands. Markets crash, we lose customers that go out of business, employees leave for reasons that have nothing to do with our decisions.

We can blame ourselves for these outcomes, or perhaps for not seeing them on the horizon. But every one of us have limitations. We need the serenity to accept that. Just as blaming others for failure won't help us make necessary changes, blaming ourselves won't help us reconcile with the unchangeable new landscape we've entered.

"Insight to know one from the other"

While we don't want to fool ourselves with self-limiting beliefs, we also can't beat ourselves up by ignoring our true limitations. Where do we gain the insight to know one from the other? One way to get clarity is by soliciting feedback from others.

Sometimes we can be blind to our own capabilities and limits, while others see them more clearly. Soliciting input from more than one person helps ensure we are getting objective information instead of trading our bias for another's.

Another way to visualize what's within our control is to consider our track record. If we have not controlled similar outcomes in the past, is there any reason to expect it to be different now? This time might be different or not. Repeated issues give us an opportunity to learn from the past and make adjustments for the future.

Whether it is through training ourselves, delegating to others, or enlisting new systems to support our success, we may not change a set outcome, but we can change the similar ones to come.

Receiving the gift

I believe that Barry Sanders is the greatest running back to ever grace a football field. During his heyday in the '90s, I never missed a game when the Detroit Lions were on TV. Moreover, if the Lions were on offense, I didn't partake in bathroom breaks or trips to the kitchen for snacks. Why the fanaticism?

I knew that following any snap of the football, number 20 could slip past a befuddled defender and run the length of the field for a touchdown. Of course, he also might get tackled for a two-yard loss, but not before eluding multiple opponents with his inertia-defying lateral moves and quickness.

During an era in which every football player seemed to have a trademark touchdown dance, Sanders would walk over to the referee and graciously hand him the pigskin. Years later, fans voted Sanders' humble and unassuming tradition as the #1 touchdown celebration of all time—beating out Jamal Anderson's 'Dirty Bird' dance and even the 'Ickey Shuffle' of Elbert Wood.

Sam Sen is a close friend whom I worked with for many years, including as part of the incident response team at BP following the Gulf Oil Spill. Sam is unflappable. Even during times of great stress and anxiety, he exudes calmness. He possesses serenity. One time, Sam and I were discussing the humility of Barry Sanders.

As we did, Sam shared some advice he had received from his father. Sam's dad discouraged his son from being influenced by what others thought of him. He told Sam that he should not make it part of his identity whenever someone praised him or criticized him. It should not make him proud or defeated. Instead, he should hold it in his hands and appreciate it for what it is—a gift.

We can choose to view just about any circumstance in the same way. Failures should not define who we are. They are a gift.

Successes likewise do not inflate our importance. They are a gift.

Receive them. Hold them. Appreciate them for the gifts they are. But do not let them become the shapers of your identity.

Blame this permission slip

In the spirit of Liz Gilbert, I'm giving you a permission slip. Instead of writing it on the back of an old shopping list, I've written it in a book. You have permission to be creative, to take the initiative. The permission slip reminds you not to let blame hold you back. Not that blame won't be there, but now you know what to do with it.

As business and marketing guru Seth Godin says:

> *Everyone who runs a marathon gets tired. There are no books called "How to run without getting tired." That's because you can't. The thing is, to finish the marathon, all you need to do is find a place to put the tired. Not avoid it; merely put it somewhere.*

So, it's not that blame disappears all of a sudden. What changes is that you do not let blame culture convince you to stop running. You finish the marathon anyway.

People will try to use blame against you. You recognize that you will still want to blame others. But now you know where to put it.

You can blame this book.

It can be the lightning rod for the resentment that arises after a failure or mistake. This might seem like a silly mental exercise, but is it any sillier than blaming someone who is only partly responsible for a problem or not accountable in any way?

Radiating frustration

Buddhist teacher Pema Chödrön shared a story from a meditation retreat she attended. She noticed a man sitting nearby who kept making a clicking sound. As the tranquility of her meditation was repeatedly interrupted, Chödrön became increasingly frustrated.

After one of the sessions was complete, she decided she would muster the courage to confront this rude guy who was ruining the experience for the rest of the participants. As Chödrön was about to approach him, the man left. But the clicking sound remained. It was then she realized a radiator was the source of the offending noise.

This changed everything. In a second, her anxiety vanished.

The clicking wasn't an insensitive or obnoxious gesture. It didn't come from a selfish individual. It came from an inanimate object with no ill intention. In fact, the radiator had no intention at all.

The Buddhist nun had an epiphany. She was the one projecting inconsideration on this man. The transgression was all in Chödrön's head. What if this is true most times?

When someone's doing something that frustrates us, we assume that's their intent. This is very common in traffic, where we can't communicate with other drivers—except with obscene gestures. So we make assumptions. But what if we believe others have no ill intent toward us? Can we be more forgiving toward them? And ourselves?

We need more heretics

In 2001, a series of videos by Rob Bell—a pastor in Grand Rapids, Michigan—propelled him to fame. Each video was about 15 minutes long, but each seemed to upend preconceived notions Christians had about their faith, their God, or themselves.

People bought the DVD series to share with friends or at small group meetings. Sunday school classes employed it as an informal teaching. Pastors even used the videos to kick off their sermons.

The appeal transcended denominations. Bell was more than a megachurch pastor. He had become a global phenomenon—writing multiple books, gaining influence, and growing his audience.

That is until he published one book in particular: *Love Wins*.

Part of Bell's attraction was his edge. He contradicted beliefs people had held for their entire lives by explaining the original context of biblical messages and how folks had misapplied those messages to their modern lives. This was fine when he discussed how we love our neighbor or spouse. It was a whole other story when he applied it to a bedrock belief in the concept of Hell.

In *Love Wins*, Bell probed the modern interpretation of Hell. He laid out the biblical scriptures describing the location—weeping, gnashing of teeth, a fire that always burns. Bell explained where each of these characteristics was derived from. Then he asked whether any of this meant non-Christians were sentenced to always and forever spend the afterlife in eternal torture and suffering.

Bell asserted it did not mean this at all. Eventually, love wins. Eventually, everyone spends eternity with God.

Immediately, the Evangelical community decided Bell had gone too far. Pastors, theologians, and other religious leaders denounced him. They removed his books and videos from their curriculum, libraries, and sermons. He was labeled a heretic.

Then Bell did something surprising. He didn't back off and make his message more palatable for the mainstream Evangelicals who were his audience. Instead he doubled down.

He realized a portion of his previous audience was ignored by fundamental teachings. There were many who had a hard time reconciling what they heard from church leaders with what they saw happening in the world around them.

These believers weren't interested in judging and condemning others. They didn't want to assume they already had all the answers. They tried to wrestle with the mystery. They needed a heretic.

Rob Bell embraced this role.

After a time in the 'wilderness', he was uplifted by influential names like Oprah Winfrey, who invited him as a guest on her *Super Soul Sunday* television program. Bell later joined Winfrey and a list of thought leaders on her *The Life You Want* tour.

Since then, Bell has continued to tour and release best-selling books. There's a debate as to whether he might've been more successful by returning to his Evangelical audience. But if he'd done that, his current audience of disillusioned Christians and agnostics searching for meaning would not have been served.

When you don't wait for permission, people will ask, "Who do you think you are?" We need confidence to stand in that moment and trust in our own vision, to not make ourselves so small that we fit into the preconceived box that society has prepared for us.

Rob Bell knew who he was. Do you?

Plowing ahead

Once we've moved beyond using blame to motivate people, we need to replace it with something else. I once heard a proverb, "Put the thief's hand to the plow." It meant that you shouldn't expect a thief to stop stealing. Put his hands to work on something worthwhile.

In the same way, we can't expect people to control their blame habit without putting something else in its place.

Instead you can provide positive reinforcement for the values you support and the goals you expect to accomplish. In addition, I'm going to share a number of tools in the next chapter.

We've mentioned data that shows leaders want their employees to be engaged. This is the ideal way to maximize each employee's contributions and the value created. Leaders are also looking for the innovation, creativity, and productivity that are the results of that employee engagement.

Minimizing blame helps immensely with all of this. It provides the psychological safety necessary to gain engagement from your employees and its attendant benefits.

Presented below are a few more practical suggestions for how you can instill a new, healthy culture in your workplace:

Feedback and candor

Annual reviews are not enough. The needs of today's ever-changing market require work teams to be flexible and agile. Multiple, shorter iterations are often more successful than longer, traditional project cycles. This means ideas should be moved to prototype quickly, and feedback should be solicited earlier and more often.

Build feedback loops, reviews, and testing into your projects. Don't turn these into automated status updates where everyone goes through the motions. These should be demonstrations or critiques of something created by the project team.

Leadership must do more than simply provide feedback, they should actively solicit input and suggestions from their teams. Provide your employees with the opportunity to give feedback about leadership, communications, systems, processes, and resources. Just be sure to show appreciation for the answers, even if it isn't positive. A poor reaction to negative feedback ensures the end of a honest critique in the future.

On that topic, all the feedback in the world is worthless if it isn't genuine. A psychologically-safe workplace encourages a culture of candor. This doesn't mean people are ruthless with their words. It does mean they feel free to speak honestly and won't withhold their opinion merely to avoid hurting people's feelings.

Establishing clear expectations

In our workplace, we define expectations with the acronym CEO—meaning Clearly, Early, and Often. Let me show what I mean:

Clearly: Expectations should paint a clear picture of your goals, and what success looks like. Use hard numbers, if possible, and establish a timeline for completion.

Early: It's best to set expectations before a project launches. Otherwise, the team can go off-track before it's barely out of the starting gate, or lose crucial opportunities for traction.

Often: Set milestones to check on progress. Waiting until a project's completion doesn't allow for adjustments to be made. If you realize expectations weren't accurate at an early milestone, this will enable you to pivot to more appropriate expectations before you waste effort or lose momentum.

Root cause analysis, not witch hunts

When people see the main goal of an analysis is to suss out what happened—examining the circumstances, decisions, information, systems, and processes that contributed to failure—instead of going a witch hunt, they'll have greater confidence to take calculated risks and contribute more significantly.

Focusing on solutions and prevention

Analyzing a failure does no good if its insights aren't used to prevent the problem from recurring. By instituting that knowledge into the company and making improvements that help avoid similar failures, employees gain security in decisions in the future.

Learning and growing

In fact, if you put the previous two suggestions into practice, then analyzing failures and applying solutions is the perfect opportunity for individuals and teams to learn and grow. This progress is incredibly gratifying and contributes to employee satisfaction and a healthier work culture.

Empowerment

Making the team part of the solution gives them ownership of how things are done. They gain familiarity with the new tools, processes, and systems implemented—accelerating adoption and change.

Habitat for Humanity is known for its generous contributions to new homes and home restoration for those who otherwise couldn't afford it. The houses are not free, though. Habitat requires the recipients to spend as many as 400 sweat hours on their new home. They give the reasons for this policy:

> *Sweat equity is an exciting cornerstone to the Habitat ministry, designed to meet essential objectives: partnership, pride in homeownership, and development of skills and knowledge.*

Allowing your teams to contribute sweat equity in the improved culture has a similar effect.

Partnership

By working together to build a better culture, your teams become tighter-knit. Teammates get to know each other and understand what their coworkers value in a healthy work culture.

Pride

There is an inherent pride in helping build a new and better culture.

Development of skills and knowledge

The experience is valuable, and the work helps each contributor develop new and valuable skills they can bring to the greater organization.

These principles can help you establish more psychological safety within your work environment. I'll use the final chapter to share more tools for establishing a culture beyond blame.

12

"It's a basic human tendency to seek clarity and closure by simplifying a complex continuum into two categories."

Adam Grant, *Think Again*

Tools for a Blame-Less Culture

When is my driverless car allowed to kill me?

Imagine you're in a driverless car. Everything seems to be going smoothly until an elderly woman using a walker steps out into your path. There's no time to stop. To your left, a semi-truck sits idle, blocking any exit in that direction. To your right the sidewalk is lined with elementary school children awaiting their bus ride.

Should your car continue forward and kill the frail old lady knowing she probably has fewer years remaining than the children? Should it swerve to the right and kill the kids because they haven't contributed as much to society yet, and maybe never will? Or should the vehicle choose to save both the woman and the schoolchildren by swerving left and slamming you face-first into the truck?

This isn't a judgment call your futuristic car will determine in the heat of the moment. Long ago a programmer made all these decisions and encoded them into an emotionless computer.

And it's not a new problem, or even a car problem. It's actually a popular thought experiment called the Trolley Problem.

In this philosophical dilemma you're a trolley operator about to kill five people standing on the tracks ahead. If you intervene and switch to a different track, the vehicle will kill just one unfortunate person on the new route. Thus, the only possible result of your action (or inaction) is the trolley kills either five people or one.

To assess how folks evaluate no-win scenarios like this, variables are introduced to the equation. What if it's a blind man on the track? Or your mom? A prisoner or a politician? Holding an umbrella or holding a gun? Thin versus overweight? What happens to the group of five if you change their gender, race, or immigration status? It's quite revealing to see how a person answers each differently.

Introduced in 1967 by philosopher Phillipa Foot, the Trolley Problem has seen a revival recently with the advent of driverless cars like those from Tesla. The difference now is that unknown software developers in Silicon Valley are coding their own answers to this moral conundrum for you.

How should a driverless vehicle react in any of the scenarios above? Should it factor in a potential victim's age or health? What about prison record, credit history, or contribution to society? There are articles full of opinions on this, but there's only one problem.

These scenarios rarely exist.

It's almost impossible for a car to choose, because it's more likely to have a myriad of possibilities and then try to navigate a solution amongst them. The dilemma makes for great philosophical debate, but life rarely boils down to easy choices—the old lady or the kids. Even so, the simplicity of such a choice is seductive.

Similarly, after a failure, we're tempted to reduce our options to a clear binary: We blame others, or we blame ourselves.

In the emotionally-charged aftermath of a mistake or failure, it seems reassuring to find someone to blame, even if it is ourselves. But, ultimately, our goal shouldn't be comfort. We should seek an understanding of what went wrong to correct it and avoid the same failure in the future.

When we blame ourselves or another individual, we deny other possibilities by limiting ourselves to two options. The reality is there is a full spectrum of possibilities to learn from.

For example, many individuals (or even teams) may have shared responsibility. The problem might have to do with the system, not a person. The issue may have been circumstances out of individuals' control, or flawed decisions may have been made because inadequate data was provided. Perhaps the training was deficient.

Open yourself up to the breadth of possibility.

Prison culture at GM

By the '80s, General Motors had a huge quality problem. Japanese automakers had captured the U.S. market with an emphasis on quality delivered through their practice of *kaizen*—a philosophy of continuous improvement. American car manufacturers just couldn't match the efficiency and standards of their foreign competitors.

To even the playing field, GM began an initiative to prioritize quality manufacturing. There was one small problem—it wasn't working. So, in 1986, the carmaker did something very unusual. They hired an anthropologist named Elizabeth Briody.

For three months, Briody camped at a vast GM plant that manufactured semi-trucks, buses, and medium-duty trucks. She observed that the plant's primary emphasis was to keep the assembly moving. Workers did everything they could to avoid stoppage. They knew if the line were interrupted, they'd be blamed for the holdup, and their boss would yell at them.

Running out of parts was the most common reason for stopping the assembly line. To avoid being blamed, the workers would hide stashes of items that frequently ran low. They'd even trade for these parts with other departments. As you can imagine, these habits created an inventory nightmare. There was no documentation for this informal trade network. It resembled a prison bartering system, operating off the books and behind the scenes.

No matter how much GM talked about quality, their overall issues would not improve as long as the old habits of blaming undermined the new initiative.

Itches, scratching, and calamine lotion

Performing an objective analysis of the failure is almost guaranteed to provide better solutions than blame would. Still, we consciously or subconsciously accept blame as our standard mode of operation.

We do this partly because blame scratches an itch created by the emotional baggage of failure. After a problem occurs, tension needs to be resolved. That's the itch blame alleviates. But, like scratching poison ivy, it does nothing to heal the issue. Instead, our actions makes the situation worse by spreading blame around.

After a failure, realize the instinct to 'scratch that itch.' Then, instead of mindlessly reacting, take the time to objectively analyze the failure instead of looking for someone to blame.

Awareness is a calamine lotion for blame.

It soothes the itchiness, so we don't scratch away. It allows us to focus on something other than the itch of blame. Now we can pay more attention to the root cause of the issue. We can troubleshoot and perform a forensic analysis of sorts. Rather than defensively reacting and making a difficult situation even worse, we can defuse our emotions and engage our problem-solving skills instead.

Welcome to a new world

Once we're more aware of blame, we're ready for tools to help us mitigate blame in our teams. We can learn to avoid the interpersonal resentment that destroys psychological safety at work, and assess the true causes of isolated and repeated problems.

This helps us step into a new world—a blameless world.

Well, that might be overstating it. We're still human. Blame will creep back in. But at least we have the tools to deal with it.

We can say "no" to harboring resentment and allowing it to turn our workplaces into toxic wastelands. We can refuse to scapegoat individuals who aren't wholly responsible for the failure just because they are convenient or different from us. We will recognize there is no point in resenting ourselves and tearing down our self-image—or letting anyone else do that to us.

Instead, as we move beyond blame, we will value ourselves and value others. We'll work to create an environment where everyone is empowered to engage in their work and bring 100% of themselves and their contributions to the table. We will build trust with one another. This psychological safety will drive more innovation. It will help our team's creativity flourish. And all of this will impact the bottom line through increased productivity and reduced loss.

Our work culture will be more attractive to top talent. They will be utilized more effectively and retained more readily.

Are you ready to create such a workplace? The following stories and tools are not an exhaustive list, but they're a great place to start your journey to that verdant green valley beyond blame.

Shaping the habits that shape culture

In Chapter 10, we discussed Charles Duhigg and his book *The Power of Habit* in which he divided habits into three essential elements.

The first element is the 'cue.' This is the trigger that initiates a habit. An example could be me walking by my kitchen pantry. Next is the 'routine.' This is the activity that the cue triggers. So, my cue of walking by the kitchen pantry triggers me to rummage for food. And finally, we have the 'reward.' This is the payoff. Rummaging through my pantry leads to a reward of eating a snack—usually something salty or sweet. Each element reinforces the other to galvanize the habit. The innocent cue is a reminder triggering a mindless routine which pays-off in a tempting reward.

Just as these elements work together to create the habit, they can also be dissected to buck the habit. Duhigg explains this with a helpful framework. He begins by identifying the routine: What is the behavior you want to change? In my case, I want to stop rummaging through the pantry when I get home from work.

The next step is to experiment with rewards. Ask how you can adjust your routine to deliver a better reward. Try several ideas, and you might find something you enjoy more than the original reward. I decided to replace my unhealthy snacks with drinking flavored electrolytes. I discovered I wasn't necessarily hungry during these times but could usually benefit from hydration. The drinks were full of flavor and satisfied my craving for something delicious.

Duhigg's third suggestion is to isolate the cue. Pinpoint exactly what triggers your routine (the location, time, emotional state, person, or the immediately preceding action). This takes awareness, of course, but you should be able to identify the cue the next time you find yourself falling into a bad habit.

I realized my pantry raids typically happened as soon as I got home after work. This helped me introduce another reward. Now when I get home, I spend time playing with my kids.

The last step in the framework is to have a plan. Decide how you want to respond to future cues. If your habit occurs at a specific time, plan to do something else at that time or set a phone reminder so at least you're aware that an unfavorable cue might be coming. Then replace the reward, and adjust the routine if that helps.

To stop my snacking, a plan might sound like this: When I walk past the pantry, I will fill a glass of water with electrolytes and drink it. Or, when I get home from work, I will spend time with my kids until we start making dinner.

Let's apply this framework using Elizabeth Briody's example from GM. When there was a stoppage, the boss would yell at the workers until they avoided stoppages at any cost. This cued other habits that created inventory issues and negatively affected quality.

GM's plan might've looked like this: "When the assembly line is stopped (cue), we will inquire about the cause and identify recurring issues (routine). We'll acknowledge and show appreciation for those who bring attention to the issue and help find a solution (reward)."

By isolating the cue, identifying and changing the routine, plus experimenting with rewards—GM could have taken what was viewed as a negative (assembly line stoppage) and turned it into an opportunity to improve their systems and processes so they could achieve their goals of higher quality manufacturing.

If you want to explore Duhigg's framework and apply it to your personal and work life, visit charlesduhigg.com/how-habits-work/ for more details on how to manage habits successfully.

Building creative confidence

The Palo Alto-based design firm IDEO has a history of innovation and revolutionary design. In 1980, they developed the mouse for Apple's game-changing new computer, the Lisa (which had the first graphical user interface on a personal computer). The very next year, IDEO's cofounder Bill Moggridge led the design effort of the first notebook-style computer for GRiD Systems.

With a powerful influence across nearly every industry and continent, the company is considered a leader in design thinking and team collaboration. Moreover, the award-winning creativity is consciously fostered in a workplace worth emulating.

Two of IDEO's principals—David Kelley, a cofounder, and his brother Tom, a partner—have written a book about how to do just that. It's called *Creative Confidence*. And that's a great goal in and of itself, establishing a work culture that promotes creative confidence within every employee.

According to the Kelley Brothers, building creative confidence empowers employees to realize their full potential. It enables them to innovate in a fun and rewarding way. It exposes the truth that each of us is the creative type. And, by sticking to a methodology, new approaches and solutions are generated—enabling individuals to do and create amazing things.

The Kelleys are also fans of the late Gordon MacKenzie (profiled in Chapter 9). They agree that we all embrace our creative genius early in life, but our identity is stolen from us by societal pressures. This fear of being judged causes us to avoid the risk of creativity in business. In a *Harvard Business Review* article they stated, "You cannot be creative if you are also censoring yourself. Half the battle is to resist judging yourself."

Ready to give it a try? Here are tips to build creative confidence:

Think divergently and creatively

A lot of our decision-making is based on convergent thinking. We gather existing ideas, weigh them against each other, and choose our favorite from that group. We may spend some time generating ideas, but they are typically top-of-mind thoughts that come quickly.

Unfortunately, this low-hanging fruit probably comes easily for the competition too. How do we get to the breakthrough ideas that others haven't even considered, let alone chosen?

Divergent thinking creates opportunities for loosely-connected ideas to build off of one another, leading to unusual and creative solutions. It enables us to go deep and wide in our thinking.

One tool for divergent thinking is a mind map. To make one, write the central topic or challenge in the middle of a large sheet of paper or a whiteboard, then circle it. An example could be "Wife's birthday party."

Outside of this circle, jot down connections to this topic—things like "Host away from home" or "Her favorite TV show as a theme." See which secondary ideas spur tertiary ideas like "Ask a friend to host" or "Rent a hotel ballroom." If an idea becomes a hub for many others, you can draw a circle or square around that focal point or underline the hub idea.

Try to come up with as many ideas as possible. Don't edit or censor yourself. Divergent thinking is not about idea critique; it is about idea generation. Focus on quantity first, and don't worry about quality until you have exhausted as many possibilities as you can.

Encourage and accept constructive feedback

Creative confidence in teams requires members to feel free to experiment. This may be needed early in a project when success is uncertain, and results may be far from perfect. Experiments need feedback, which can be challenging to listen to and accept without our egos interfering.

This is where IDEO uses the tool "I like/I wish" to introduce constructive feedback into the experimental processes that lead to innovation. I find it helpful for group reviews in small teams when you want to solicit and provide a helpful critique without squashing the creative confidence of your teammates.

Set the tone for the session by explaining the "I like/I wish" method. For example, a facilitator can request helpful feedback on their presentation, asking participants to share positive feedback by starting sentences with "I like…" ("I like that your exercises were engaging and tied directly into the theme of your presentation.")— and provide critical feedback with "I wish…" ("I wish the presentation ended on time, so there was more time for Q&A.").

The facilitator notes each statement as participants take turns sharing. This documents the feedback and allows the participants to clarify their comments. The facilitator should not dispute feedback, making the participants defensive, but should listen and take notes.

You have the prerogative to request all "I like" statements before gathering the "I wish" statements. Or you can choose to receive whichever feedback participants choose to provide in random order.

Eliminate hierarchy to improve idea flow

In groups with differing levels of authority—where an executive may be interacting with frontline workers—it can be helpful to reduce awareness of the hierarchy before the group participates in a creative exercise. This will allow more junior group members to contribute without feeling suppressed by a manager or leader.

A good way to break the ice is with the Nickname Warm-up. This exercise allows participants to assume a persona outside the company's authority structure.

The facilitator provides a hat or bowl filled with pre-filled name tags. (Names that lend themselves to humor are most effective, as teams tend to produce their best work when having fun.) The names can be inspirational or silly but should evoke a lot of personality— like Mr. Magnificent, Junebug, Dr. Lion Heart, or Honky Tonk.

The participants each pull a name tag out of the hat and wear it for the rest of the event. The facilitator then tosses a ball into the group. Whoever catches it then introduces themselves in character, using the new nickname, and tells a short, improvisational story about the origin of their nickname as a child. Once they finish their story, they toss the ball to another participant until everyone has introduced their new persona.

These suggestions are just a start. With planning, you can foster a work environment where everyone feels empowered and positive. Visit the Kelleys at creativeconfidence.com/tools/ for more ideas.

Setting expectations

Blame at work can be the result of a poor beginning. Often people are blamed for things they didn't even know were expected of them. This is because these expectations were not stated explicitly until after they were not met—which is not very helpful. This isn't just an ineffective management technique; it's also unfair to the individuals saddled with the blame.

Here are a few basic steps to help set proper expectations and avoid resorting to blame afterward:

1. Establish clear goals

The established benchmark for creating goals is known as SMART (which stands for specific, measurable, achievable, results-oriented, and time-bound). By using SMART goals, you ensure expectations are clear. This avoids confusion, so your team members do not miss the project's objective, timeline, or expected results.

2. Define a process to reach the goals

Start by asking the person you're giving responsibility to how they'd achieve the goal. It may also be good to ask them how much of your help they would want for defining the process. Do they appreciate a more hands-on approach or prefer more autonomy? Even if they wish for independence, they should be willing to share their process with you. Just be sure to give them the appropriate amount of time to work that out themselves.

3. Put it in writing

It's not enough to verbalize your expectations. Write it down. This isn't just to have a document to refer to later if results aren't met. Writing the expectations helps clarify your communication. It allows others to understand exactly what you want and provide feedback or suggestions. It ensures there is agreement on expectations. Ask them for honesty so you can work through any differences in opinion.

4. Be approachable

Even if expectations are established early on, changes happen. When adjustments are needed, others should feel comfortable discussing them with you. If you seem too rigid or unavailable, they may decide it's preferable to put off dealing with critical issues until it's too late to do anything about it.

5. Establish how goals will be measured

Decide with others how you will measure the expectations. If they don't seem measurable, then you probably didn't use SMART goals. Make sure you have a system in place, even if it's just a spreadsheet or a form, so that you can track results. Schedule a regular cadence for updating the data. This will ensure it's accurate. And, remember, inputting data along the way requires very little effort compared to searching through a Tower of Babel after too much time has elapsed.

By setting clear and agreed-upon expectations early in a project, you improve your opportunity for success while giving others the respect they deserve instead of the blame they don't.

Visualizing the child

One of the reasons we blame others is that we lack empathy for them. Without this understanding, we may make unfair assumptions about their intentions or character. This makes it easier for us to see them as blameworthy. And as long as we believe they deserve the blame, it will be difficult for us to avoid scapegoating them.

How can we combat our judgmental attitudes? In his book *Positive Intelligence*, author and executive advisor Shirzad Chamine recommends a game he calls "visualizing the child." He explains the premise for this exercise with an example most can relate to:

> *If you go to a playground and watch five-year-olds play, you will probably feel instant empathy and caring for these total strangers... You can use this fact to shift your brain to feel empathy and caring for yourself or others.*

To increase empathy for oneself, Chamine suggests visualizing yourself as a child. Go back in time and see yourself playing a game, petting a puppy, or drawing with crayons—any innocent activity you recall. It might be helpful to find an old photo of yourself as a kid.

To gain empathy for others, the exercise is similar. You envision your colleague as a child before they became weighed down with the trappings of adulthood. Imagine their facial features and hair. How did they carry themselves as a child? What causing them to smile? Imagine them with the fresh confidence and joy of childhood.

Though it sounds like a solitary practice, Chamine encourages us to give his technique a try in the middle of the workday:

> *You can do this in the back of your mind even while you are interacting with [your colleague] in a meeting. It will instantly impact how much empathy you feel.*

When we imagine those around us as children, we make fewer assumptions about their intentions. We learn to have empathy for the flaws in their character.

Visualizing the child helps us see past our presumptions and beyond superficial appearances. We understand people for who they actually are—their essence.

An accidental discovery

Management researcher Amy Edmondson was helping to lead a project studying medical errors in multiple hospitals. Her specific focus was about the potential effects of teamwork on the rate of mistakes committed.

She assumed that the most effective teams would have the least medical errors. This didn't seem like a stretch. As expected, there was a tenfold variance in results based on teamwork.

But Edmondson didn't anticipate that the correlation was the exact opposite of her hypothesis: better teams made more errors (not less) than weaker teams. Then she uncovered a revelatory fact—better teams didn't make more mistakes.

They reported more.

Through additional observations, the research verified that the groups exhibiting better teamwork also talked more openly about mistakes and ways to prevent them.

Edmondson realized that this healthy interpersonal climate resulted from psychological safety, as theorized by organizational development titans Edgar Schein and Warren Bennis while they were professors at MIT in the '60s.

Everyone can achieve psychological safety

Is psychological safety just a feel-good nice-to-have? Not really. Edmundson has written two books, *The Fearless Organization* and *Teaming*, which detail the importance of cultivating psychological safety in medical teams and in any workplace.

Every industry contains the interpersonal risk that influences the effectiveness of teams—and the organization as a whole—challenging their success and potential. Edmondson demonstrates that psychological safety is not dependent on specific personalities or a level of team chemistry, but is something every leader and teammate can and should work toward.

In addition, her research debunked the common assumption that fear is an effective motivator. Instead, it inhibits the learning and cooperation that foster effective teams and allows them to perform analytical thinking, creative insight, and problem-solving.

Edmondson lays out the principles of psychological safety and provides a survey for measuring it. As you can see below, the survey is short and direct. Members of your team rank each statement on a scale of 1 (strongly agree) to 7 (strongly disagree):

1. If you make a mistake on this team, it's not held against you.
2. Teammates can bring up problems and challenging issues.
3. Teammates often accept others for being different.
4. It is safe to take a risk on this team.
5. It is easy to ask other members of this team for help.
6. No teammates deliberately undermines my efforts.
7. My unique skills and talents are valued on this team.

Any results that are 1 or 2 are considered high scores. As results descend, this indicates a significantly unhealthy—and potentially toxic—work culture. If you want to assess the level of psychological safety in your team, you can use these questions to develop your own survey, or visit Edmondson at comparativeagility.com/capabilities/psychological-safety-assessment/ to participate in her study.

Make trust personal

Patrick Lencioni's seminal book *The Five Dysfunctions of a Team* shares a modern fable of a team that has been underperforming and is led through a series of exercises by their new CEO.

Deadlines are missed, and the team struggles to work together. The story eventually shows how a lack of trust is the foundation for the team's dysfunctions. Lencioni argues that vulnerability is the key to developing confidence.

And leaders, he says, must go first:

> *Trust lies at the heart of a great team, and a leader must set the stage for that trust by being genuinely vulnerable with his or her team members.*

Vulnerability requires us to admit a mistake we have made or to ask for help. This isn't natural for a lot of leaders. It can feel like a sign of weakness. But admitting mistakes and asking for help makes us more relatable to our colleagues.

Conversely, when leaders pretend they never make mistakes, team members sense dishonesty. This not only makes the leader less relatable, but it calls their sincerity into question. How can the team member trust a leader who is not honest with them?

One way to develop more trust is to increase understanding. Lencioni recommends what he calls a "Personal Histories" exercise. Each team member answers the questions below:

1. Where were you born? Where did you grow up?
2. How many kids in your family? Where are you in birth order?
3. What was the biggest challenge you overcame in childhood?

When you use the exercise, two things happen. First, trust is improved. It takes vulnerability to answer personal questions. In essence, each person thinks, "I've got nothing to hide, so I'll tell you something about myself."

Second, by gaining insights into their teammates, people realize they share similarities. Understanding each other on a fundamental level means we're more likely to give the benefit of the doubt instead of assuming someone's behavior indicates malice toward us.

Death of a sales opportunity, in review

> *The actual point of blameless postmortems is to remove the fear of looking stupid, being reprimanded, or even losing your job with the ultimate goal of encouraging honest, objective, and fact-centric communication that leads to better future outcomes.*

Atlassian Incident Management

For decades, after the completion of a military event, the U.S. Army performed ineffective but commonly-used performance critiques. These usually involved a commander delivering a lecture focused on errors that occurred and changes to be made. These often resulted in divisiveness and created tensions between departments.

Then, in the 1970s, the Army developed the AAR (After Action Review). In contrast to the performance critiques, AARs are more egalitarian. They are participatory conversations among colleagues instead of a dressing down by an authority. Input is welcomed from everyone, helping to develop greater unity instead of division.

Instead of being a lecture, AARs tell a story. This taps into our ability to absorb narratives and learn from them—something humans have done since we developed language.

The end result? AARs promote positive organizational change.

The following outline includes aspects of a Blame-less Autopsy to add to the effectiveness of performing an AAR within a business.

Before the Review

Get buy-in from leadership

If your organization hasn't yet performed a blame-less autopsy, it requires a cultural shift. Be sure to meet with leaders and share why you want to do this review. Be clear, not just about the benefits but also about the challenges, and the necessity of their support.

Set the tone

With your team, be clear that the review is not about casting blame. Criticism should be constructive. Encourage "I" statements instead of "you" statements. For example, instead of saying, "You sent me the contract at the last minute", participants could say, "I got the contract late in the process, which made it tough to finalize without errors."

Emphasize the goal is learning

Remember, this is not a witch hunt. The focus is not on who but on what happened, why it happened, and how the same mistakes can be avoided in the future.

During the Review

Answer four specific questions

What did we expect to happen?
What did everyone expect to happen as a result of doing the project? By providing this context, the team understands everyone had good intentions at the start. This framing emphasizes the intention to work as a team and support each other in success.

What happened?

This isn't just an opportunity to gather varying perspectives. The AAR team should agree on the story being told. Leadership should not impose their will in this case. Individuals should work through their differences to stack hands on what really happened.

What was the difference between our expectations and reality?

It's not enough to identify the delta between what you expected and what actually happened. An AAR should also explain why this delta exists. Without learning the right lessons, the exercise is impotent.

What can we change next time?

Finally, those lessons learned must result in real effective change. That's the purpose of an AAR. You must apply your new insights, so the same mistakes aren't made again.

Celebrate the successes

Even a failed project has some wins within it. Celebrate what went right. Maybe a partial goal was met. Perhaps new information was discovered. At the very least, the failure created an opportunity to learn. Whatever positives can be attributed to the project should be highlighted before focusing on the mistakes.

Accept mistakes and failure

If failures aren't acceptable in the current work culture, soliciting honest information from your team members will be challenging. Remove the fear of admitting mistakes by focusing on the need for brutal facts to identify the root cause and learn from it.

Capture the results

Not only should the review document what happened and why. It should also summarize the results of the failure.

What was the impact of the mistakes made? Did it negatively affect revenue, customer experience, team dynamics, or the culture? These details will emphasize the importance of the review process without resorting to blame.

Establish the timeline

One last tip: Resist the urge to ask who did what. Instead, focus on when events occurred. This emphasizes learning the facts, rather than trying to fix blame on an individual.

After the Review

Generate action items

In the end, this process should contribute suggestions for improving and avoiding similar mistakes and failures in the future.

Be sure to solicit suggestions during the process and formalize them into a document that can be submitted to leadership.

Involve the whole team in brainstorming potential solutions to the issues that caused the failure. Assign action items to individuals with a timeline for when they should be completed.

Don't switch to blaming

After you complete a Blame-less Autopsy, don't use that information against individuals. If you do, having another in the future will be impossible. Workers will realize quickly that anything they share in the post-mortem process can be used against them later.

Measure success

Be sure to set a timeline and measurements for success. When will changes be made? What results do you expect to see due to these changes? Include both qualitative results (like improved customer experience in reviews) and quantitative results (20% improvement in customer lifetime value due to reduced churn).

Know today what killed you in the future

The only problem with After Action Reviews is that they occur after. What if you could predict issues and mistakes before they happen? This is the idea behind a project pre-mortem.

First proposed by cognitive psychologist Gary Klein in 2007, a pre-mortem allows a team to imagine their project has already been completed. This enables them to identify risks and opportunities at the outset of a project. It's the complete opposite of a post-mortem. Instead of explaining what killed the patient, your team imagines what has the potential to kill him.

To do this, start right away. Soon after your team is briefed on the project plan, the leader informs them the project was an utter failure. Individuals then spend time detailing whatever reasons they imagine contributed to the demise of their project—which, in reality, they have yet to execute.

One of the benefits of generating fictional but believable reasons for failure is the freedom to mention problems that team members might otherwise avoid for political reasons. The imaginative aspect of this exercise provides a bit of shelter for such suggestions.

Each member is asked to read one previously unstated reason from their list until all the differing predictions are documented. After the exercise is completed, the project manager reviews the list and develops a strategy to strengthen the project plan against all of the potential threats.

Vicious Spirals vs. Virtuous Cycles

> *When organizations develop positive, virtuous cultures, they achieve significantly higher levels of organizational effectiveness—including financial performance, customer satisfaction, productivity, and employee engagement.*
>
> Emma Seppälä and Kim Cameron,
> *Proof That Positive Work Cultures Are More Productive*

Clinical psychologist Dr. Henry Cloud coauthored the bestseller *Boundaries*, which has sold over 2 million copies and become a bedrock for therapists and counselors. It establishes how individuals can take responsibility for their feelings and actions but not the emotions and behavior of others. This simple principle becomes very challenging in the mire of relationships, especially unhealthy ones.

Applying these concepts to the business world, Cloud wrote a follow-up entitled *Boundaries for Leaders: Results, Relationships, and Being Ridiculously in Charge*. In this book, he describes the 'Death Spiral of a Leader.' It consists of three Ps:

First, we believe failure is Personal: "A bad thing happened to me because I am in some way bad." Then, we believe it is Pervasive: "Everything is (and has been) going badly." Finally, we believe failure is Permanent: "It is always going to go badly."

This death spiral makes us unnecessarily blame ourselves while simultaneously creating a sense of helplessness. The spiral can seem inescapable when the first step into the mad descent is believing that bad outcomes result from our character flaws.

Cloud encourages leaders to audit their thinking and realize that failure is never any of the three Ps: personal, pervasive, or permanent. Once you understand this, you can break out of the death spiral, overcome failure, and discover success again.

Cloud encourages leaders who desire to move beyond blame to counter the three P's by observing, logging, and refuting.

The way to pull yourself out of a death spiral is to become aware of your thinking patterns, first through self-observation and then, secondly, by writing your thoughts down in a journal. Finally, review each sentence and identify counterarguments and facts to refute, one by one, the falsity of the claim.

While explaining this approach, Cloud emphasized that life is a movie, not a scene. "Every great movie has crisis scenes in it."

This is where we do have control. We may not control a crisis's individual scenes, but we create the narrative those scenes fit into.

The award for Best Editor goes to you

You control the editing of your life.

You don't run the cameras or control all the actors, but you take the footage and give it meaning. What happens to us is momentary, but the stories we tell ourselves stay with us. Losing a sale, losing a job, or losing an entire business (all of which have happened to me personally) do not define your life. Each one is a scene.

How you insert them into the movie of your life is up to you.

As Garr Reynolds says on his blog, *Presentation Zen*, editors are the unsung heroes of film. But if we take a closer look, even those of us outside of film can learn valuable lessons from their creative work. Whatever the medium, the key to great storytelling is cutting out the superfluous, keeping only what helps the overall narrative.

We aren't in control of our circumstances, but we are—as Cloud maintains—"ridiculously in charge" of how we tell our stories.

Blame occupies a massive amount of psychological space in most organizations. This is because blame is not simply a cycle in two dimensions. It has a depth that can be descended. Blame creates a vicious downward spiral.

We talked earlier about how blame destroys trust. It also creates shame and insecurity. Distrust, shame, and insecurity generate more blame—which creates more distrust, shame, and insecurity. And the vicious spiral repeats, descending further and further down.

But when we remove blame from the equation, we create space for something even more significant—grace.

We are more likely to trust those who give us grace. This trust creates a healthier sense of psychological security. That security gives us the confidence and courage to share ideas and take creative risks. This creative output encourages us to trust each other and give grace.

And the virtuous cycle repeats, rising higher and higher up.

Epilogue

A Blame-Less Future

Why does this book matter? Is it a big deal if people continue to use and abuse blame? Is blame culture really that toxic?

I can imagine a future where we blame less. This isn't a utopia where everyone is nice to each other, and no one is ever mean. It's not just motherhood and apple pie. Breaking the blame habit has real-world benefits that translate into bottom-line results.

Fewer scapegoats. More accountability

When I talk about eliminating blame, one of the biggest hang-ups people have is a fear that their teammates or employees will avoid their responsibilities and there will be no accountability.

In reality, the opposite is true. When blame is prevalent, so is scapegoating. Leaders wield blame as a weapon, using it to protect their status, income, and reputation. In the process, they damage status, income, and reputation of their victims. In the end, blame makes it harder to hold the right people accountable for mistakes.

You can more readily identify individuals who contributed to a failure by remedying blame culture. You can hold team members accountable for their mistakes and take steps to avoid or mitigate errors in the future.

Fewer pseudo-solutions. More problem-solving

Not only does blame make it difficult to hold the right people accountable, it's also harder to identify systemic issues responsible in a failure. As we discussed earlier, blame creates a pseudo-solution. It's a distraction masquerading as an answer. Most blaming does not solve the actual problem. It simply relieves the anxiety and pressure created after mistakes and failures.

When a team doesn't rely on blame, they have to dig deeper into the cause of the problem to find an actual solution. This means identifying decisions, processes, systems, and events that may have contributed to the issue. The primary benefit is you are much more likely to solve the problem and avoid it recurring again in the future.

Less fear. More creativity and innovation

Fear of blame hinders your team's creativity. It short-circuits your organization's ability to innovate. Blame reduces our tolerance for risk. Risk management is valuable, but the quest to eliminate risk pushes everyone to follow the safest route possible. This means no one suggests anything that is new or unproven (the breeding ground for creativity and innovation).

Blame reduces idea generation. It discourages sharing of new thoughts and encourages individuals to fly under the radar.

A blame-less culture is more collaborative due to greater trust and confidence in each other. It promotes the cross-pollination of ideas. If team members aren't worried about apportioning blame or credit, they're more willing to share their thoughts. Not only is idea generation improved, but teams are more inclined to adopt new innovations from teammates and build on them.

Less oppression. More engagement

Blame is often used to protect status. Those with status and power often wield blame against those without it.

The original scapegoats often had no status: poor beggars, the diseased, foreigners, prostitutes, and criminals. Ironically, the people with enough status and power to make the decisions that actually led to failure were hardly ever blamed as the scapegoats.

When scapegoating is gone, there's a greater focus on problem-solving among the entire team. Together they can improve the product, service, process, customer experience, and work culture.

Instead of fearing they will be blamed for whatever goes wrong, team members see they are a valuable resource for solving it. While blame cultures alienate those without status, blame-less cultures invite everyone to contribute and engage.

Fewer toxic workplaces. More grace

Ultimately, the prevalence of blame in the workplace creates the toxic environments we read and hear about, often in the aftermath (or sometimes the foreshadowing) of a business or moral failure.

Those responsible are not corrected. The root cause of these issues is not identified, let alone addressed. Teams lose their edge as creativity and innovation wain. All of this creates disengagement as employees are disconnected from solving issues in an environment where each person is busy covering their ass.

Conversely, blame-less teams are more resilient. They generate more goodwill from their teammates because they offer each other grace instead of blame. This helps develop *esprit de corps*—that sense of pride, camaraderie, and belonging in high-performing teams.

In fact, the best way to develop grace in your team, according to David DeSteno, a psychology professor at Northwestern University, is to cultivate gratitude, compassion, and pride. Teams that displayed these three markers also demonstrated greater grit, determination, and higher performance results than teams without. They were more patient, more willing to invest in each other, and less lonely.

If ever there were an antitoxin for workplace culture, it is grace.

Blame beyond the office

If you haven't picked it up yet, I want to point out something else. The principles of this book do not apply solely to the workplace.

Becoming blame-less is about life in general.

Our personal life is full of the potential for blame: the anxiety of failure and unmet expectations; the hurt of another's actions or words; the gnawing sense inside that we don't measure up.

The resentment and anger—against others and ourselves—builds to a crescendo, boiling over into a desire for revenge. And, unfortunately, we occasionally succumb to this temptation.

This is the dark matter in the life of a flawed human being.

We're all flawed.

The issue is: How do we not allow blame to control us?

Psychologist John Gottman, considered a founding father of relationship counseling, identified four behaviors that are toxic in relationships: criticism, contempt, defensiveness, and stonewalling. He called these The Four Horsemen and asserted they significantly contributed to destabilizing marriages. And all of them can originate from unaddressed blame and resentment.

I hope you can take the principles of this book and apply them to your life, in general, not just at work.

We can strive to be responsible and hold each other accountable without resorting to blame. The world would be a better place with fewer scapegoats and more attention given to solving problems dispassionately. Any environment will benefit from reducing or eliminating The Four Horsemen of toxic relationships.

We can move away from acts of blame like hate, violence, shame, oppression, and vengeance. Instead, we can embrace acts of grace like love, charity, encouragement, equality, and forgiveness.

Our homes, neighborhoods, town halls, and our churches can become even greater forces of good in our communities and for the world at large. We can transform our interactions in-person and on social media—bringing civility to our disagreements, and healing the polarization of our politics.

This may sound like a vision of grandeur. But it's a vision of what is possible when we take a stand and start going beyond blame in one place that we always have complete control over:

Ourselves.

When you cease to exist, then who will you blame?

Bob Dylan

About the Author

Dustin Staiger is the principal partner at The People Brand. There he unearths, for each of his clients, the essence of their business. This establishes both a culture that attracts their best employees and a brand that attracts their best customers.

Dustin has consulted Fortune 100 firms, and—with his team at The People Brand—has provided consulting and training for clients such as British Petroleum, ConocoPhillips, and Align Technology.

Starting his career as a designer, Dustin is an award-winning marketer who has made creativity his hallmark. The highlight was helping a struggling retailer transform their failing business into one that thrived while branching into new locations, reigniting the owner's passion and vision that had nearly been snuffed out.

Dustin developed communications for the recovery effort to the BP Deepwater Horizon Oil Spill, serving on a team with Secretary of Energy Stephen Chu, and producing reports for President Barack Obama. He helped develop a program to verify the competency of oil and gas companies to avert future disasters.

In addition, he worked with global commercial furniture giant Steelcase to share their research regarding the impact of workplace design on innovation and productivity.

Dustin is married to Tammy. Along with their three children, they call North Texas 'home.'

Acknowledgements

I want to acknowledge my wife Tammy, who has been in unwavering support of me—even when I chose to write an entire book about blame. (Who does that?) You picked me up. Thanks for listening to all my quirky theories and bringing them up whenever I didn't take my own advice while trying to find someone to blame. You kept me grounded.

Abbie, Grant, and Derek: You each give me hope that the future will be better. That gives me a reason to keep writing.

Mom and Dad, you gave me the freedom to choose my own path. Your love and support gave me a priceless foundation. I told Mom I'd write a book she could read someday. Here it is.

A special acknowledgment to my editor Fredrick Haugen: You inspired me to reach deeper and aspire to create something big enough to match the message in my heart. Thank you for helping my idea take shape, find its voice, and exceed expectations technically and emotionally.

Mr. Chenoweth, you saw the artist in me and guided me to my passion for creative work. Thank you for teaching us backwoods Oklahoma kids to create our own masterpieces. You are a scholar and a gentleman.

Melody, Marilyn, John, Paul, Linda, Jenna, Martha, and Matt: Thanks to our creative team and the inspiration it has given me. The 'umbrella of grace' and other aspects of team culture show me that the hum-drum of work can be redeemed into something beautiful.

Seth Godin, thank you for being the voice who has poked and prodded me throughout the years. There is much of your influence in this book and my persistence to write it. It was in your workshop that the idea for *Blame This Book* was born. This would never have happened without you, Scott, Louise, Wes, and Sam.

Taylor Harrington and the team at Groove: I am so grateful for the community and technology you have created that helped me get this book done.

Thank you, Avraham and Covington, for keeping the innovative spark alive and fanning it back into a flame.

Mark and John, thanks for giving me the space and latitude to work on this. Your encouragement, feedback, and friendship are invaluable.

References

Articles

"Case file: The murder of Meredith Kercher." (2022, August 18). Forensic Science Society.

"Shame vs. guilt." (2021, October 28). Brené Brown.

"Get the corporate antibodies on your side." (2014, July 23). Harvard Business Review.

"Lori Loughlin and Mossimo Giannulli receive prison sentences for admissions scheme." (2020, August 21). NPR.

"How successful people handle toxic people." (2022, October 12). Forbes.

"The survivors left behind." (2020, January 6). Columbia Medicine Magazine.

"How businesses fail to get the best from software." (2021, February 11). The Irish Times.

"Toxic culture is driving the great resignation." (2022, January 11). MIT Sloan Management Review.

"Psychological Safety Assessment." Psychological Safety.

"Man became a millionaire after finding a copy of the declaration of Independence in the frame of an old painting he bought for only $4 in 1989." (2020, July 4) Vintage News Daily.

"How to stop the blame game." (2014, July 23). Harvard Business Review.

"Alleged gunman tells police he wanted to rescue children at D.C. pizza shop after hearing fictional internet accounts." (2016, December 5). The Washington Post.

"How to negotiate out of shutdown stalemate? 'getting to yes' author has advice." (2019, January 11). Here & Now.

"How habits work." (2017, November 20). Charles Duhigg.

"CEO secrets: Don't fire staff for making mistakes." (2021, September 28). BBC News.

"This chart shows how quickly college tuition has skyrocketed since 1980." (2016). Business Insider.

"Reclaim your creative confidence." (2014, August 1). Harvard Business Review.

"How an infamous spitting incident saved Charles Barkley's career." (2020, April 4). Sportscasting.

"When the myth of voter fraud comes for you." (2021, December 21).The Atlantic.

"Gorilla killing: 3-year-old boy's mother won't be charged." (2016, June 6). CNN.

"Moving from blame to accountability." (2016, August 16). The Systems Thinker.

"Amanda Knox reveals why she lied about details in Meredith Kercher Case." (2020, December 2). Peoplemag.

"Amy Edmondson: Psychological safety is critically important in medicine." (2019, November 12). AAMC.

"After gorilla death, try empathy–not blame. "(2016, May 30). CNN.

"The secret to storytelling is in the editing." (2013, January 7). Presentation Zen.

"Proof that positive work cultures are more productive." (2017, May 8). Harvard Business Review.

"The economics of quiet quitting and what we should call it instead." (2022, September 13). NPR radio show Planet Money.

"An icon, not an idol." (2022, September 9). Andrew Sullivan. Substack.

"Olivia Jade Giannulli 'wasn't angry' at her parents after college admissions scandal: 'I didn't see the wrong in it.'" (2020, December 8). Peoplemag.

"How the Buddhist metaphor of 'The second arrow' can help you be nicer to yourself." (2020, March 10). A Lust For Life.

"BP's clumsy response to oil spill threatens to make a bad situation worse." (2010, June 1). The Guardian.

"ABC News' Jennifer Ashton on her ex-husband's 2017 suicide: 'I was feeling ... this is my fault.'" (2019, May 1). Peoplemag.

Films

The Wizard of Oz. (1939). Metro-Goldwyn-Mayer.

The Incredibles. (2004). Buena Vista Pictures.

The Shawshank Redemption. (1994). Castle Rock Entertainment.

Books

Bell, R. (2013). *Love wins: A book about heaven, hell, and the fate of every person who ever lived.* HarperCollinsPublishers.

Bock, L. (2015). *Work rules!: Insights from inside Google that will transform.* Twelve.

Brown, B. (2012). *Power of vulnerability: Teachings on authenticity, connection, and courage.* Sounds True, Incorporated.

Chamine, S. (2016). *Positive intelligence: Why only 20% of teams and individuals achieve their true potential and how you can achieve yours*. Greenleaf Book Group Press.

Cheever, S. (1994). *A woman's life: The story of an ordinary American and her extraordinary generation*. W. Morrow.

Collins, J. (2001). *Good to great: Why some companies make the leap ... and others don't*. HarperBusiness.

Dekker, S. (2006). *The Field Guide to Understanding Human Error*. CRC Press.

Deming, W. E. (1986). *Out of the crisis*. MIT Press.

Duhigg, C. (2014). *The Power of Habit: Why we do what we do in life and business*. Random House.

Dweck, C. S. (2017). *Mindset: Changing the way you think to fulfill your potential*. Robinson.

Ehrenreich, B., & Estrada, S. (2010). *Bright-sided: How positive thinking is undermining America*. Picador, H. Holt and Company.

Gilbert, E. (2015). *Big Magic: Creative Living Beyond Fear*. Penguin Publishing Group.

Grant, A. (2021). *Think Again*. Penguin Publishing Group.

LeeYohn, D. (2018). *Fusion: How integrating brand and culture powers the world's greatest companies*. Nicholas Brealey Publishing.

Lencioni, P. M. (2007). *The Five Dysfunctions of a Team: A Leadership Fable*. John Wiley & Sons.

Lencioni, P. (2012). *The Five Dysfunctions of a Team: Team Assessment*. Jossey-Bass.

MacKenzie, G. (1998). *Orbiting the Giant hairball: A corporate fool's guide to surviving with grace*. Penguin.

McGregor, D., & Cutcher-Gershenfeld, J. E. (2005). *The Human Side of Enterprise*. McGraw-Hill Professional.

Orwell, G. (1945). *Animal Farm*. Secker and Warburg.

Peters, T. J., Peters, & Waterman, Jr, R. H. (1982). *In search of Excellence*. Harper & row.

Pink, D. H. (2010). *Drive: The surprising truth about what motivates us*. Canongate.

Pressfield, S., & Dolmage, J. (2017). *Do the Work!* W. Ross MacDonald School Resource Services Library.

Rollo, M. (1996). *Psychology and the Human Dilemma*. Norton.

Tolle, E. (2018). *The Power of Now: A guide to spiritual enlightenment*. Hachette Australia.

Ury, W. (2015). *Getting to Yes with Yourself: And other worthy opponents*. Element Books.

Wink, W. (1999). *The Powers That Be: Theology for a new millennium*. Doubleday.

Podcasts

"Repairing our Country." *Making Sense*, Episode 296. Sam Harris.

"False Confessions." *Speaking of Psychology*. APA.

Videos

"Esther Perel on Workplace Dynamics." SXSW channel, YouTube.

"Choosing Falling over Failure." Simon Sinek channel, YouTube.

"Charles Barkley: Spitting on a little girl changed my life." Graham Bensinger channel, YouTube.

"The power of believing you can improve." Carol Dweck, TED.

"Your elusive creative genius." Elizabeth Glibert. TED.

"The argument for trouble." Mark Modesti. TED.

"Your body language may shape who you are." Amy Cuddy. TED.

www.ingramcontent.com/pod-product-compliance
Lightning Source LLC
Chambersburg PA
CBHW060844280326
41934CB00007B/907